It Could Happen to You

D1403226

It Could Happen to You

Diary of a Pregnancy and Beyond

Martha Brockenbrough

**Andrews McMeel
Publishing**

Kansas City

Versions of many of these essays appeared originally on MSN WomenCentral,
Microsoft's online program located at womencentral.msn.com.

02 03 04 05 06 VAI 10 9 8 7 6 5 4 3 2 1

Library of Congress Cataloging-in-Publication Data
Brockenbrough, Martha.
    It could happen to you : diary of a pregancy and beyond / Martha
Brockenbrough.
        p. cm.
    ISBN: 0-7407-2685-4
    1. Brockenbrough, Martha—Health and hygiene. 2. Pregnancy—Popular
works. 3. Pregnancy—Miscellanea. 4. Pregnant women—Biography. I. Title.

RG526 .B757 2002
618.2—dc21

                                                                2002074470

ATTENTION: SCHOOLS AND BUSINESSES

Andrews McMeel books are available at quantity discounts with bulk pur-
chase for educational, business, or sales promotional use. For information,
please write to: Special Sales Department, Andrews McMeel Publishing, 4520
Main Street, Kansas City, Missouri 64111.

For Adam, who fills my heart, and for Lucy, who makes it soar. And for my mom and dad, who gave us everything.

Contents

Acknowledgments   xi

Introduction: First Comes Love, Then Comes   xiii
  Marriage

Chapter 1: Before It Was Too Late   1
What Do Baby Chickens Eat?   1

Chapter 2: The First Trimester (Now It's Too Late)   5
Testing, Testing: One, Two, Three . . .   5
Mom and Dad, I'm Not a Virgin   9
The Garfunkel Syndrome   12
The Worst Day, Ever   15
What's Happening to Me?   18
How to Tell Your Boss You're Pregnant   21
Be Still My Beating Heart   25

Contents

Chapter 3: The Second Trimester ... 28

This Is a Kick ... 28

The Awful Truth about Pregnancy ... 31

Talking about Sex with Strangers ... 35

The Name Game ... 39

The Dad-to-Be's Chapter ... 42

Finally! Some Good Advice ... 45

Maternity-Clothes–Minded ... 49

Chapter 4: The Third Trimester ... 53

Where Babies Come From ... 53

Everything a Baby Really Needs ... 57

Womb with a View ... 60

On Childbirth and Cheese-Steak ... 64

The Secret Fantasy of All Pregnant Women ... 68

Letters to a Baby on the Way ... 72

A Mother's Work Is Never Done ... 80

Momsomnia ... 83

Chapter 5: The Birthday ... 88

I Remember the Day You Were Born ... 89

Chapter 6: The Fourth Trimester ... 98

The Houseguest from Hell ... 98

Welcoming Wishes ... 102

Parentnoia ... 107

The Baby Boom ... 111

Contents

Naked Bliss	114
What's That Smell?	117
How to Dress a Baby	121
Dads Don't Mind (Another One by Adam)	125
Becoming a Mother	128
How to Change a Diaper	132
Mother Love	135
A Day in Cold Hell	138
A Taste of Baby Blues	141
Chapter 7: Good Times and Guilt	147
I've Found My Inner Martha	147
We're Bad Parents. Really Bad	153
Lucy in the Sky with Diapers	157
Uptown Girl	160
The Ever-Changing Baby Face	163
My Breast Friends	167
Solid Food, Solid Sleep	170
The Great Baby-Clothes Debate	175
Why I Quit My Job	181
Chapter 8: More Than We Can Chew	188
The Tooth Hurts	188
A Guy's Guide to Baby Holding	193
Back in the Running	197
Two Plus One Equals Enough	202
I Love Lucy and She Loves Me	206

Contents

Uncle	211
The Model Child	215
The Thing with Lucy's Mouth	218
Lucy on the Loose	222
The Myth of Mother Knows Best	227
Chapter 9: Getting a Life	231
The Leather Anniversary	231
How to Put a Baby to Sleep	236
The Age of the Cheerio	242
Pets vs. Babies	246
Lucy's First Word	249
Lucy Learns a Lesson	253
Was I Ready for This?	257
Clash of the Parents	263
Lucy Is One	267

Acknowledgments

Just as no child grows up happy without the love and support of many people, no book reaches readers without the help of many hands. I would like to thank everyone who has helped me give birth to this one, especially my anesthesiologist. Oh wait. I didn't have one this time.

But seriously.

I couldn't have written this without my husband, Adam. He's my best friend, and the best person I know. Also, he got me pregnant in the first place. Without that, there would be, quite literally, nothing to say on this subject.

Thanks, also, to my parents, brothers and sisters, and in-laws for continuing to speak with me after I shared deep family secrets with the world. Even more, thank you for holding Lucy on Sunday nights during the howling hours. My arms

Acknowledgments

were breaking, and you saved me. For this and many other reasons, I love you all.

I also could not have done this without our nanny, Laramie, who works wonders with Lucy, with me, and even with an early draft of this book.

Nor could I have done this without my friends at Microsoft, who let me keep this public journal in the first place. I'm also grateful to the readers who shared similar thoughts and their own parenting stories.

I owe a large debt to my friend Sheryl, who designed the cover for this book and also taught me that great mothers don't have to wear headbands and penny loafers. And to Stoobie, who makes technical difficulties on the Internet feel like just another ladies' night out.

Thank you also to Elaine and Morgan, who blazed a trail and helped illuminate some dark spots for me, and to Nan and Tanya, who believed in me and helped make this dream real.

First Comes Love, Then Comes Marriage

I started keeping a diary the day I turned eight.

"Dear Diary," I wrote. "Today is the happiest day of my life, because I got *you,* my diary."

The day after I turned eight, I stopped keeping a diary. Childhood happiness makes lousy journal fodder. Little did I know that twenty-two years later, I would be full of a child of my own, and full of the kinds of stories that do make great diary entries. This time around, I had something much better than happiness to write about: comic relief.

Here's how it all came about.

Fast-forward fifteen years from my happiest day. I was twenty-three, working as a low-paid intern at a mediocre newspaper in Tacoma, a city known by some as the armpit of Seattle. In this armpit, I met the man I would marry.

I didn't realize this at the time, though. I was busy dating the suave and charming guy who sat next to him. To me, Adam was just the friendly, ponytailed geek who drove a burgundy Mercury Topaz with a pink door. Eventually, I stopped dating Adam's neighbor, finished two long years at the newspaper, and moved on to an even lower-paying job someplace else. Anything to get out of that job, I figured.

My move almost became a way out of work entirely. At my new job, I came close to getting fired for union rabblerousing. I got the hint when my boss clacked her long, red fingernails on the desk and said, "Maybe you'd be happier working someplace else." Feeling utterly shattered, I mustered my courage and called Adam, who had left the armpit newspaper for a much better job at Microsoft. He had an opening for a boring temporary job that involved entering Web sites into a database and rating their content on a scale of one to five. Tedious work for twice the money. It sounded perfect.

After a few months working together, I started to think of Adam as more than that ponytailed geek, due in no small part to the fact that he finally had cut his hair. The more time I spent with him, the more he made me laugh. When he accidentally deleted ninety-five records I had entered into the database, he bought me ninety-five sticks of gum. A former airbrush T-shirt artist, he also drew my name up on his whiteboard in big, bubble letters next to a tropical sunset. If I had wanted, he would have drawn a nude woman driving a Harley across a skull. We had our first date at a junkyard, so that we could retrieve some things from the trunk of his car (why it was there is another story). And the day after that, as I was scrubbing my toilet, I thought, *"I will probably marry him."*

Of course, I did not say this to anyone but the toilet brush. I had no plans for marriage that I cared to talk about with a real person. I'd had my heart smashed before, and I would rather be alone than feel that way again. So, it was a fine surprise, after I had dated Adam for a year, that I liked him better then than I had at the beginning of our relationship. In fact, I loved him. I realized this one summer weekend as we were standing outside a bed-and-breakfast in the San Juan Islands, watching a once-in-a-lifetime comet blaze across the sky. For the first time in years, I felt nothing but happy, lit up by a love just as brilliant and rare as that comet.

This feeling of bliss lasted until we started planning our wedding.

I quickly became a disgruntled bride. This happens when you try to plan an outdoor, Jewish-Catholic, mid-May wedding ceremony in Seattle, where rainfall is measured in yards. Anyone would have been broken after experiencing an eight-hour shopping trip for napkins with her future mother-in-law, followed by a discussion with my dad about why I didn't want to stand on Astroturf during the ceremony. At the time, I thought, *"Hey. I should be writing this stuff down. Anyone who's ever had to plan a wedding will think it's hilarious."* But I didn't quite have the courage. And now most of the funny stories are gathering dust, along with the negatives of our wedding pictures.

When I got pregnant two years later, I knew that having a baby was going to supply me with laughs to last the rest of my life. Not only would I finally have to break the news to my parents that I was no longer a virgin, I would also get to see what I'd look like if I were smuggling a turtle. I would find out, once and for all, whether it is truth or urban legend that pregnant women feel driven to eat pickles. And I might even finally get a chest worth talking about.

I wanted to be able to remember these things, so I started writing them down. I hope you enjoy them, and as you're reading, remember: The same thing could happen to you.

Chapter 1

Before It Was Too Late

My husband and I are either going to buy a dog or have a child. We can't decide whether to ruin our carpet or ruin our lives.

—Rita Rudner

Hey, Adam. We already have a dog and two cats. The carpet is shot. Let's have a baby!

What Do Baby Chickens Eat?

A few weeks before Adam and I got married, his cat started barfing. A lot. We could be eating dinner or watching TV, or stuffing chocolate-covered nuts into wee boxes because we thought wedding guests actually cared about such things, when his cat would pause, hunch up, and start making this awful noise. It sounded like this: "Cachork, cachork, cachork, cachork," and then "Splak." And with that, the cat would cough up a scary, wet heap, which Adam would have to clean, because the sight of barf makes me barf. In return for Adam's chivalry here, I get to clean the toilets. This is all in our prenuptial agreement, along with the "no minivan, ever" provision.

The cat, whose name—appropriately—is Spot, sullied our carpet for about two weeks straight in the days leading up to the wedding. Spot had always been a bit of a hurler, but in the past, he expelled hairballs, not food. And it never went on more than a day or so. Adam and I grew worried enough to take Spot to an emergency vet on a Sunday, where we spent $242 to find out they had no idea what was wrong. The vet advised us to feed Spot chicken baby food, and off we drove, silently fretting about our boy.

Spot had been Adam's cat for many years by the time we became a family. Even though Spot welcomed my dog to the fold by pooping aggressively outside his litter box, thus costing Adam his security deposit, and even though Spot ushered my cat, Lily, into the family by punching her face every morning, we love him. He's a bastard, but he's *our* bastard. And so, just days before the wedding, I found myself worrying that Spot wasn't going to make it. We wouldn't just be having a wedding ceremony; we'd be having a cat funeral. I felt awful for Adam, but I was ready to be the strong and supportive wife, the source of comfort and hope. Just as long as I didn't have to clean up any puke.

As we drove past a grocery store near home, I gently suggested that we pick up some chicken baby food for Spot.

"I am not feeding him chicken baby food!" he snapped.

It was the first time I'd ever seen Adam really mad, so it surprised me and scared me a bit, considering how close we were to the wedding, and how I'd already put down a nonrefundable deposit on the cake. I decided to drop it. Adam could be irrational about this one point. He had earned it. Just as long as I still didn't have to pick up any puke.

The next day, Adam and I went for lunch at a little teriyaki joint near work. It's in a strip mall next to not one but two pet food stores and a birdseed shop. As we were walking into the restaurant, Adam looked at the pet food bonanza before us, sighed, and said, "I guess we can get him the chicken baby food."

It took me a minute to figure out why Adam was bringing this up now.

"Adam," I said, "what do you think chicken baby food is?"

"You know—scratch," he said. "Corn, oats. I don't know what's in that stuff."

Then it hit me: Adam thought chicken baby food was what you feed baby . . . chickens! Trying not to lose bladder control, I explained that chicken baby food was actually pureed chicken. It comes in jars. "*Human* babies eat it," I said.

Days later, I married Adam. Spot lived to see the wedding. He liked the chicken baby food just fine. Three years have passed and Spot's with us still. He barfs only occasionally. And Adam, bless him, cleans it up.

Even now, whenever I see baby food jars in the grocery store, I get the giggles. Adam is a great husband and a great friend. And now that he knows what chicken baby food is, he's that much closer to being ready to be a father.

But am I ready to be a mother? This is probably the hardest question I've ever had to answer. I don't know of any way of knowing for sure, other than listening to my heart. I feel as though I'm standing on the edge of a high dive, wondering whether to jump. Will it hurt? Probably. Can I take it? I think so. Will I be glad I did? About that, I can only guess.

I went through a similar dialogue before I got married, and I'm very glad I made that choice. Like marriage, this decision will change my life forever. But unlike marriage, one of the key players won't have any say in the matter. And I'm not talking about the cat, here. I'm talking about the baby. Children don't ask to be born. And as a parent, part of your job is to make them glad they're here—without cheating and buying toys and candy all the time. My own parents managed to succeed in this, but I saw the toll it took on them. Their hair turned gray. They never wore fashionable clothes. And they made us eat the Vegetable of the Week.

Can I do all of that? Adam says he's up for it. And lately, as much as it surprises me, I'm feeling the same way.

I just hope there isn't a lot of barf.

Chapter 2

The First Trimester (Now It's Too Late)

Life isn't a matter of milestones but of moments.
—Rose Fitzgerald Kennedy

For a matter of moments, the first trimester sure lasts a long time.

Testing, Testing: One, Two, Three . . .

As soon as Adam and I started swinging on the love trapeze without a net, I started to think I was pregnant. When we went out to dinner with a group of friends, I chose not to have a glass of wine, just in case.

"What are you, pregnant?" one of them asked.

"No," I said. "I just don't feel like any wine tonight."

That was such a lie. I always feel like having a glass of red wine when I'm at a dimly lit restaurant eating goat cheese and arugula. Even though I don't know how to pronounce arugula, and even though I don't want to think about how they get the

5

cheese out of the goat, the remote possibility of a pregnancy was enough to make me pass on the wine. This answers the "Do I want a baby?" question somewhat. I can say definitively that I want a baby more than I want wine. Granted, that's not going to win me a Mother of the Year trophy, but at least it is a bit of hard evidence that I wasn't just kidding when I gave Adam the green light.

I read once that people used to test for pregnancy by injecting urine in a rabbit. If the rabbit died, that meant you were pregnant. Later, I found out that it wasn't the toxic pee that killed the rabbit. It was the scientists, who needed to off the bunny to check her ovaries for a reaction to the hormone in the pee. Unfortunately, I didn't know any scientists with a spare rabbit, so I had to get my own pregnancy test.

Because I still have some issues regarding human sexuality left over from seventh grade, I was too embarrassed to buy the test in the local drugstore. I wanted to browse in private, not with people who were looking for hemorrhoid cream. Also, I didn't want to give the check-out clerk anything to gossip about in the staff room. *Did you see that shifty-eyed woman buying pregnancy tests? She looked like a twelve-year-old!*

Thank goodness for the Internet. I went to an online drugstore and started examining their offerings. There were several kinds of tests to choose from, and the prices ranged from $6.99 to $16.99, although some came one to a pack, some came two to a pack, and some came three to a pack.

After doing some basic math, I was looking at anywhere from $5.50 to $8.00 per test. Did I want a cheap test? What would that say about me? That I was cheap? Or that I was merely saving money for this child's college education? Also, was there a difference between the cheap test and the expensive test? Was one more accurate? More important, did the more expensive one include a rabbit that I'd have to feed?

I must have clicked around for an hour before I finally decided on a mid-priced, double-test. That, and a new lipstick for me, just in case we were going to have to try again later with the trapeze. A few days later, my test arrived in the mail. I was too jittery to tell Adam I had ordered one, and when I saw the package in the lobby of our building, I quietly took it upstairs and into the bathroom. I unwrapped it and followed the instructions on the box. Then I waited. After a couple of extremely long minutes, a little blue line showed up in the window on the test stick.

Bingo.

"I'm pregnant," I thought. *"I'm pregnant. Pregnant. Man, I really hate that word, pregnant. Isn't there another way of saying it?"*

I looked at myself in the mirror, and saw that I had a huge smile on my face, a smile that said, *"I'm having a baby."*

Then I put on some of my new lipstick and went into the living room to tell Adam. I shook all over as I told him that I'd just taken a pregnancy test, and that it was positive.

"Are you sure?" he said.

"Yeah, I think so," I said. "But I have another test. Should I take it?"

Adam, who now claims he was just trying to be scientific, insisted I try again. The results were the same the second time around. And they were the same the third time around, in my doctor's office.

It's so hard to believe. Inside of me is another human being. Right now, this person is just a collection of cells that don't even look like a baby. But someday soon, these cells will be a real, live child in my arms, looking to me for comfort, protection, love, support—everything, really. Most turning points in my life, I have not been able to recognize until afterward. This one, though, is clear. I don't know how life is going to change, but I know it will never be the same.

When I was a kid, I used to think about the children I would someday have. I saved my dolls for them. When I was working for peanuts as a reporter, skimping on food and haircuts for myself, I still set aside money every month for their college educations. Last summer, before I formally acknowledged I was ready to have a baby, I even made a spreadsheet with all my favorite names for boys and girls. As I think about it, I'm realizing I'm a dork for making a spreadsheet. More important, I'm realizing that all the other moments of my life have led to this moment I am living now.

Am I ready? I think I am. It's probably just the hormones that are making me cry.

The First Trimester (Now It's Too Late)

Mom and Dad, I'm Not a Virgin

It's one thing to get pregnant. You get to do that in the privacy of your own home. If it makes you feel better, you can even tell the pets to wait outside for a few minutes. Once you are with child, you face the much more difficult task of telling your parents. But let me back up a minute.

It was the right thing for me to pass on the wine, because Adam and I went from "It sounds like the right thing" to the little blue "You're pregnant!" line in the shortest conceivable time. I almost even mean that literally, but to spare Adam's dignity, I'll say that it took just the right amount of time. In any case, neither of us expected things to happen so fast. We'd read all about the general problem of infertility, and we had also commiserated with close friends over conceptions that weren't happening. So, where many couples may assume they will have no problem and find out the hard way that they need a little help, we prepared ourselves for the worst.

In retrospect, this was a bad idea. If you decide you want to have a baby, you should be ready to learn that you're carrying one within two weeks of that fateful discussion. If you're really lucky, it can happen.

And then you have to tell your mom and dad.

As long as you're not an unmarried teenager, letting your folks know that they're going to have their first grandbaby should be easy. It should be fun. Everyone likes babies, right?

So I have no idea why I felt so nervous about it. Maybe because it meant I could officially no longer carry on the pretense that I was still pure. Or maybe I'm just a little odd. Heck, maybe it was just the hormones talking. How should I know? This is all very new to me, and since I had to tell my parents first or risk getting grounded, there was no one I could talk to for advice on this point.

Uncharacteristically, Adam was no help. He thought he should tell his parents, and I should tell mine. So, I devised a plan.

Back when were in the startlingly brief trying-to-conceive phase, Adam had a dream about a swarm of small children who had plunged into the ocean for an important race. One eventually pulled into the lead, and I dove in for the last stretch and accompanied her to the shore. Adam woke up laughing and felt certain this was a clear indication that we would have a girl. I thought if I gathered my family around and had Adam tell them about his dream, they would get the symbolism and share in the joy, sparing me from telling them the sordid details of the pregnancy test. Instead of appreciating the metaphor and understanding what we were talking about, my mom turned gray in the face, and my dad just blinked behind his glasses.

So, Adam said, "Martha's pregnant."

Now I had two pale parents.

"We had no idea you were trying," my mom finally said. I *knew* they thought I was still a virgin.

Since then, they've officially become excited. Thank God. Telling Adam's mother was a lot easier for me, mainly because he had to do it. Adam's mom already has nine grandchildren, so she immediately knew "Congratulations" was the right word to say in reply to the news. But because Carol never has just one word to say on any topic, she continued.

"My psychic told me just this weekend that you were going to have a baby," she said.

Later, when Adam told his brother and sisters, more details emerged. The psychic saw a vision of Carol's mother carrying a rose, telling her something special was going to happen. Carol's first interpretation was a bit more mundane: that the vision was about an upcoming bat mitzvah for our niece. Now, some people might wonder why Carol would pay a psychic to tell her about an event that had been planned for many months. I have found that it's better just to enjoy the fact that Carol has psychic friends. And I'd already seen first-hand what a fun grandmother she is, even if she doesn't want anyone calling her Grandma.

All told, our nine brothers and sisters had the best response to the news—plain and simple joy. People at work also responded happily, as did our dog. The two we haven't told yet are the pair least likely to support this new development: the cats.

Like my parents, they'll probably just look at us and blink. I'm not sure I can go through that again.

It Could Happen to You
The Garfunkel Syndrome

Even though my mother was a little slow to process the news that I'm pregnant, I have no doubt but that she will be a world-class grandmother. Just thinking of it warms the cockles of my very heart—unless that's heartburn I'm feeling.

But still, I am just the slightest bit depressed. Here's why.

Human beings are a nasty, competitive lot. If you're not No. 1, you're nobody. Well, you might be No. 2. But who cares? No one. Just ask Art Garfunkel.

You'd think that childbirth would be exempt from competition. Fat chance. Everything's a benchmark: how much weight you gained, whether you got stretch marks, how long you labored, if you used anesthesia, and—finally—how your baby scored on the Apgar.

If men gave birth, there would be trading cards handsomely emblazoned with all these fine stats. And probably one additional one: yardage. In a world where men bore children, babies would be ejected and caught in special mitts made from the hide of fierce animals. The distance would be measured, and then other men would sit behind a desk analyzing stats and compiling them into books meant to be read on the toilet. Men cannot resist this. But women give birth, and there are no trading cards. Just folklore. Which is worse, because you can never escape it, and its value does not diminish with heavy handling. In fact, the opposite is true.

And this is why I grieve: I am human, I am competitive,

The First Trimester (Now It's Too Late)

and I know there is not a chance in hell I am going to be the best mother in the world.

Why? Because my own mother already holds the title. Consider the facts:

- She had a basketball team's worth of children without anesthesia and still wears size four pants. She doesn't even need to grease her legs to get into them;
- The day she bore my youngest sister, she went grocery shopping. This was after my doctor dad tried to postpone labor by giving her an antidiarrhea pill;
- She made many of our clothes, including our prom dresses;
- We had fresh-baked after-school snacks every day;
- She heated up our towels for swimming meets;
- She has run six marathons—and won her age group for the last one; and
- She works as an elementary school nurse and spends her own money on anonymous Christmas gifts for the children Santa would have forgotten.

That's just a sampling of what she's done. She also washed our crib sheets daily and continued to breast-feed me even after I got teeth and started using them. I know it shouldn't matter that my mom did—and does—all these great things. I appreciate the fact that she's sewn me three maternity tops and removed the spills from two others. Her devotion and love gave me the greatest advantages a person can ever have.

But because I'm a lousy kid, I'd still like to claim victory in some area. Any area.

And I don't think I'm the only one who gets pangs of birth competition. Many baby books I've read make reference to the fact that American women used to be knocked out completely during labor. This gave a whole generation of baby-boomer women like my mother something to feel smug and superior about: natural childbirth. Why couldn't that have been enough for my mom? I would have really liked to own the award for after-school snacks, or maybe the size-four-pants trophy. She didn't leave a lot of mountains to climb, which means I might have to settle for "best all-you-can-eat-pudding-breakfast" honors. Adam would like that.

Why couldn't Mom, just for once, have thought of my sisters and me—and been a little more selfish?

I know the answer, of course. I used to see it every day, on the lunch-napkin notes she'd write. Or when I forgot to bring underwear to change into after swim practice, Mom thought nothing of driving an extra ten miles so that I would not be damp, chafed, or humiliated. I still have many of the notes she wrote me during the lowest times of my childhood, notes expressing her sweet, sincere—if naïve—faith in my goodness.

The answer was love. Hers had no edges, and she has more drive and energy to express it than anyone I've ever met, with the possible exception of my dog. She also had an especially convenient clause that "whoever deserved her love least needed it most." Which meant I got more than my fair share.

And I'm sure this baby will feel the love, too, darn it. My mom will be such a great grandmother that by the time this baby grows up and has a child of its own, I'm going to be in second place in the grandma category, too. How unfair is that?

Rest assured: I plan to take advantage of her industrious love as soon as the baby is born. She's already volunteered to give the baby its first bath. But I think the wee one also deserves clean crib sheets every day. And I'd like a reprise of her after-school snacks—I have to keep up my strength somehow.

The Worst Day. Ever

I will never eat meat loaf again. Never. Never, never, never, never, never. Ever! I will also never return to this Chicago restaurant called Ed Debevic's. I'd always wanted to go to Ed's, ever since my brother mentioned it on an earlier visit to see him and his wife. It's one of those places where the waiters and waitresses give you lip as they serve up reproduction kitsch classics: meat loaf, mashed potatoes.

Because we were on vacation, Adam, John, Kim, and I treated ourselves to a meal there. And because I am pregnant, I indulged in the meat loaf. Ordinarily, I'd never order something so naughty. But what, I thought, would a few more calories be? I have the ultimate excuse if I got a little porky: I am taking care of the baby. So, meat loaf it was, along with mashed potatoes and a viscous puddle of gravy. The waiter was as mouthy as I expected, and later he entertained us all by getting on the counter and singing. Adam even won a free T-shirt for knowing that Leonard Nimoy was the voice behind the rendition of "Proud Mary" that was playing on their juke-box. After lunch, the four of us walked around Chicago and smiled, despite the stiff, cold wind that was freezing our faces in funny expressions.

When we got back to John and Kim's house, I didn't feel so good. I parked myself on their couch and breathed quietly. *"Don't barf . . . don't barf . . . don't barf,"* I kept saying. I've always hated throwing up, ever since the Great Thanksgiving Folly of 1977, where I topped off my turkey bonanza with two kinds of pie and a couple fistfuls of chocolate. While I slept, dreaming explosive dreams, I cast a blanket of barf two yards wide on either side of my bed, fouling my new shag carpet and my rose-patterned comforter with matching curtains. Since then, I've lived in fear and loathing of nausea. You would too, if you saw my mother's face when she came to wake me up the morning after and found I'd gone Exorcist all over my new stuff.

Even though I have considerably more skill at barfing neatly than when I was a deep-sleeping seven-year-old, I still despise the act. I was hoping I'd be able to have this baby without getting sick. Fat chance. I made it through six weeks, and then one morning, after I had cantaloupe for breakfast, up it came. Adam and I were on the Florida leg of our vacation, getting ready for a day trip to the Everglades when I lost my fruit. I felt pretty miserable, but I put on a brave face, brushed my teeth, and went and faced the gators. For all I knew, that was going to be the only time that pregnancy got the better of me. Besides, it was just cantaloupe.

No one who has barfed up meat loaf ever says, "It was just meat loaf." All told, I coughed up sixteen times during a two-day spree. I thought I was going to die. I lay in bed, all shaky and pale, and thought, *"I'm not even going to leave a good-looking corpse."* I was so sick that I had to cancel a trip to see a good friend turn thirty. If this was pregnancy, I thought, why didn't I just get a puppy?

The Ed Debarfic's incident, as I have come to call it, so far has been the hardest part of being pregnant, although I still get sick regularly unless I start the day with a bowl of chicken noodle soup. I also get sick when I walk uphill, and when I make coffee in the morning for Adam. My friend Sheryl says she also had a horrible day before her daughter, Sofia, was born. So, maybe this is just one of those ways you're tested. If you can't take the puke, then stay out of the parenting game.

Just to be safe, though, I'm staying away from the meat loaf.

What's Happening to Me?

As the reality of this pregnancy sinks in, the books are starting to pile up. I can remember going to the home of some pregnant friends and seeing the stack of sex-ed-for-grown-ups books on their living room shelves. At the time, I felt unworthy. No way would I ever be able to read so much on a single topic. My heaviest reading back then tended to be *InStyle* magazine. At two hundred pages, it is fairly weighty. But it was nothing compared to the volume of reading my friend Heidi was doing about the baby inside of her. If she could read all those books she was ready to be a mother, and a good one. At best, I was preparing myself how to make my apartment look more feng shui.

Yet, here I am, expecting a baby, and suddenly completely uninterested in learning how to steal a starlet's look or decorating know-how, for the simple and vain reason that I can no longer stand the sight of a celebrity waistline. I went snowshoeing recently, and fellow adventurers had to buckle my shoes for me because bending over was so uncomfortable. Instead of craving glossy magazines full of thin models, I am finding myself absorbed in fat books about pregnancy. Thanks to the generosity of friends, as well as a few bookstore splurges, I have about three dozen. Before I created some rules for myself, I started to get overwhelmed. It might have been the four-hundred-page book I read in a single day that did it. After that, though, I got strict: I am only allowed to read about my current stage of development. When I was seven weeks along, I could read about the first seven weeks of pregnancy. And so on.

My main reason for this is that forty weeks seems like an eternity. I have about thirty weeks to go, and can't imagine my due date will ever arrive. When I was in first grade, the teacher marked 181 school days on the edge of the wall, running all the way around the classroom. The sun moved around the room, counting down days until none remained, and we could all go enjoy summer vacation, which I considered the single greatest invention in human history. It took forever for the sun to make this orbit. Compared to the 280 or so days of pregnancy, though, 181 school days seem like child's play.

I find I do much better when I think about thirty days at a time. Or seven, which seems to fit my attention span better. Luckily for me, there are books that break down pregnancy into digestible chunks. They're the soda cracker of gestational literature: light, snappy, and in no way nauseating. It's turning out to be a fascinating way to relate to this unborn child. During the seventh week of pregnancy, for example, my baby's jaw formed—tooth buds and all. It still doesn't have eyelids yet, which means it is staring at me. This is fine; it's keeping me on good behavior. By the ninth week, the baby had fingerprints, but has also started sucking its thumb, which would make taking fingerprints impossible for any Fetus Cops that might be patrolling my uterus. During the tenth week, the baby could squint, wrinkle its forehead, and frown—everything it needed to express disapproval at my lame jokes about Fetus Cops. And by now, the eleventh week, the baby has started to urinate. Even though it's urinating inside me, dangerously close to where I put my lunch, I'm fine with this, because there are no diapers yet to change.

Enough of that, though. The real reason I'm taking this pregnancy one week at a time is not so much that I'm afraid the end will never come. I'm doing it because I'm equally afraid that the end *will* come. I saw what the end looks like in that four-hundred-page book I read. And it's pretty scary. In some ways, I prefer the worldview I had when I was four, and my mom was pregnant with my youngest sister. One day as I looked at her bare and pregnant belly, I asked her how the baby was going to get out of her stomach.

"A very special place," she told me.

This confirmed my suspicion that the baby was going to come out through Mom's belly button, after unzipping that brown seam running down the middle of her stomach. For many years of my childhood, I thought that's what belly buttons and stomach lines were for: to act as the baby escape hatch. I've since learned that's not the case. The seam isn't really a seam, either. It's a line called *linea negra*. The fact that I know this means I'm retaining something besides water.

Now that I'm old enough to have seen pictures of this very special place my mother was talking about, doing its very special job of releasing the baby from the womb, I take some very special comfort in the fact that I have a while to get ready for this. I just wish, though, that someone would write a fashion magazine article called "Feng Shui for the Pregnant Woman: How to Rearrange Your Special Place so It Can Accommodate both a Chenille Love seat *and* a Cranium."

Then again, I'm probably not ready for those pictures, either.

How to Tell Your Boss You're Pregnant

So there's at least one chapter these books are definitely missing: the one that shows you how to tell people you're pregnant. These books often have a paragraph or two about telling your other children they're going to have to start sharing their bedrooms. But if you already have other children, you know how to tell people you're pregnant. And presumably, you're only having more children because you are no longer afraid of the ones you've got. So what's the point of that?

And it's not just your parents you have to tell; it's also your boss. I have a great boss, one who has four kids. But I had to admit I worried that even he would secretly resent the thought of losing me, even temporarily, to childbirth. I admit it. I'm a workaholic, and I didn't want to let him down, or even let him *think* that a little thing like a pregnancy would diminish my productivity. Especially not around review and bonus time.

In addition to that, Adam is one of my coworkers. We do a good job of keeping our relationship out of the public eye at work. I even got asked out on a date by someone else the week before we got married. Still, there's nothing like pregnancy to announce to everyone that a guy who works down the hall has seen you naked. Like it or not, pregnancy means you have to wear your sex life on your sleeve. Well, maybe more on the front of your shirt. Either way, though, it's enough to make a nice girl blush.

I decided to follow the twelve-week rule of pregnancy disclosure. This unwritten rule gives you three months to keep your pregnancy a secret. It came about, no doubt, because you're much less likely to miscarry after your first trimester has passed. I guess I can see why that rule exists. It gives you the opportunity to grieve in private, if that's what works best for you. But that wasn't the reason I followed it. I was too scared about the possibility to even think of miscarriage. The real reason I followed the rule was that it let me procrastinate.

Unlike the normal kind of procrastination, though, this was hard to follow through on. I've been barfing pretty much daily since I was six weeks and two days along (not that I'm counting). For a while, I lived in fear of the possibility that I'd be trapped in a meeting when I had a puke attack. What would I use? An empty cup? If I had one. The wastebasket? No way—it had a swinging top that could possibly swing the barf right back at me. My hands? Ewwww. I wanted to tell people, just so they'd get out of my way if I had to race to the bathroom. Also, it's not often life hands you a perfect excuse to get out of meetings. *"Sorry, I'm pregnant and could barf. You'll have to carry on without me."* What was the point of morning sickness if I couldn't use it?

Even that wasn't the real reason it was hard to keep the pregnancy a secret at work. The real challenge was, everyone else outside of work already knew. We'd told our families, who'd told their friends. And because no one understands what Adam or I do for a living, this became the default topic of conversation everywhere we went. Adam and I traveled to Chicago in early December for the bat mitzvah Carol's psychic predicted. My daily barfing ritual had just begun, and at a party the night before the main event, lots of well-wishers who'd known Adam since he was a little boy came up to me to touch my stomach. "You're just barely pregnant!" one of them said, reminding me that I still had a long way to go, and much nausea ahead, before I'd have anything but stretch marks to show for it.

Keeping the secret eventually felt like a burden. Right around the time I was twelve weeks pregnant, though, my boss gave my teammates and me an assignment: to prepare a series of slides outlining our future projects. And so I did. I outlined the goals I had for the second half of the fiscal year. I created three slides featuring neat pie charts and impressive growth percentages—everything I planned to get done for the next six months, morning sickness and all. The fourth and final slide featured a photograph I'd found on the Web. It was a little brown-haired baby standing on a chair in front of a computer—something like what I imagine my child will look like down the line.

"Release Version 1.0 of Adam Berliant and Martha Brocken-brough," I wrote. *"Estimated ship date, July 31."*

And that is how I told my boss a baby was on the way. It seemed a fitting way for a computer nerd to announce such news—using PowerPoint slide show software. He was both encouraging and kind about it. He even told my coworkers for me so I wouldn't have to ding a glass and make an embarrassing speech about my fertility during an otherwise unsexy meeting.

Now that I think about it, though, my slides show little I comprehend about what really is happening here. I needed three pages to talk about my job, and just one picture to talk about the life-altering work that is taking place inside of me—work that doesn't require percentages, projections, or even a plan, yet it matters more than anything else. All I have to do is take care of myself and a miracle will happen.

Maybe the more important something is, the fewer words there are to explain it. Or maybe it's just that I have a lot to learn. Something tells me it's a little bit of both. In any case, I think I'd better keep a copy of PowerPoint on hand for when I have to teach this baby about the birds and the bees. I wonder if there's a pie chart for that. The topic still embarrasses the heck out of me.

Be Still My Beating Heart

There are many things you have to learn when you're pregnant, including how to be a good patient. I stink at this. The nurse in my doctor's office has to tell me every time I visit that it's okay to go on back and produce my urine specimen as soon as I get there. Even so, I prefer to wait until I have permission. If there were hall passes, I would probably wait for one of those, too. This probably annoys the nurse, who has much better things to do than give my bladder engraved invitations to function.

My discomfort doesn't stop there. After I've labeled my sample, I wash my hands and then wipe all the water drops off the counter around the sink. If I'm going to be sullying their counters with my little plastic cup of pee, then at least I'm going to leave everything else as clean as possible. It's as though some part of me expects to win an obedience award. It's madness. Even if I do pee on command, this does not make me a dog, and no one wants to give me a cookie.

There is probably something deeply psychological about this. Perhaps I was scarred when I was a child and tried unsuccessfully to pee standing up, like my older brother. That might be reading too much into it, because Adam pees standing up just fine, yet he, too, required an invitation from the nurse before he'd leave the waiting room during our last doctor's appointment.

This appointment was a big one—our biggest yet—because

we were going to get to hear the baby's heartbeat for the first time. People have told me it's then that pregnancy starts to feel real. It's the first contact you have with your baby. I may be deceiving myself, but this pregnancy already feels real. Not only do I feel fairly awful, my pants are tight, and I'm tired all the time. If I didn't know I was pregnant, I would be afraid that I'm dying. How some people can go forty weeks and be surprised that their acute indigestion was actually labor pains is a complete mystery to me.

I am, without a doubt, in the family way. And yet, I don't think of myself as a parent. When I hear the word "mother," I think of my mom. I probably always will. Still, I was count-ing the days until I got to hear the heartbeat. And when the day finally arrived, I was thrilled. Once I had permission to be in the back of the doctor's office, I lay on the table and waited for the nurse to do her thing with the jelly and the probe. *"What's it going to sound like?"* I wondered. I grew less rational from there. *"What if we can't hear it? What if this is all some sort of mistake? What if something is wrong?"*

I felt myself get very cold as I lay on the table and waited. Then the nurse put the probe, which was covered in frigid goo, on my stomach. She slid it around for a few, slow sec-onds and then her eyebrows lifted up. Right away, I knew why. The room was filled with a steady drumming, like the sound a horse makes when it runs across hard ground. It's a dancing rhythm, filled with energy, a music that made my chest squeeze with joy.

"One hundred forty-five beats per minute," the nurse said. "It's a good, strong pulse."

Then, she moved the probe to pick up my heartbeat as well. Mine was a slower, rushing rhythm, like moving water. Together, this was the sound of two lives sharing a body, a curious, beautiful song that I could have listened to for hours while I tried to find the meaning within. Maybe this is why all human cultures have music. It's the way we bring our heartbeats outside and share them, and say, "We're alive."

And so, a little piece of the mystery of what all of this means has come into focus. There is a baby inside of me. A baby with a good, strong pulse. A baby with a heart that will someday feel the swell of love and the pinch of sorrow, and perhaps even a joy like the one I'm feeling now. Do I deserve this? Does anyone? As I think about these questions, I start to understand: Just as we don't need permission to walk into the back of the doctor's office, we don't need permission to become parents. We decided this for ourselves. And now, it's happening; it's real.

No wonder we're a little bit scared.

Chapter 3

The Second Trimester

Life is hard. After all, it kills you.

—Katharine Hepburn

And Katharine Hepburn didn't even have any children.

This Is a Kick

One of the pregnancy books I read said that "very thin" women can feel the baby kick as early as sixteen weeks, but that most didn't feel it until eighteen weeks. I really wanted to feel this baby kick when week sixteen rolled around. Not only did I really want to hit that next milestone of pregnancy, I wanted an unbiased, expert opinion that I was "very thin."

Of course, I suspected that I was not very thin. I hadn't been very thin before I was pregnant. I hadn't been very thin for quite a while, actually. When I got married, my wedding dress, which had fit a few months before, was so tight that I didn't eat any cake, although I hear it was excellent. Therefore, it was pretty ambitious of me to think that pregnancy would make me thin. But I am an optimist. And I had barfed almost every day for three months, so if anyone deserved to shed some of that useless fat she'd been carrying in her back pockets, it was me. Apparently, the baby has other plans for my back-pocket flab. I am most definitely not thinner. I have outgrown all but one pair of my normal pants, and this is a pair that barely stayed up on me when I got them.

Still I hoped I'd be one of those lucky women who started feeling baby kicks early. It would be so much fun. I could tap back, and then the baby and I could communicate in Morse code. I'd say, "Tap once if you're a boy, twice if you're a girl," and then find out for sure what color clothes to buy. I could tap out the importance of being born on time, and—more important—headfirst. This was going to be good, assuming I didn't hear dot-dot-dot, dot . . . dot, dot-dot-dot, which Adam tells me means SOS. If this baby has a ship in there, I am the one in serious trouble.

Nonetheless, when I was sixteen weeks along, I was ready to rumble. Adam and I were on a ferryboat, coming back from a romantic trip to the San Juan Islands—perhaps one of the last weekend getaways we'll take without a baby in the backseat. As we sat in the car, waiting to drive off onto the dock, I felt a twinge in my stomach. *This is it!* I thought. *I'm feeling the baby kick!*

It didn't feel quite like I expected. It was kind of sharp and painful. *"No worries,"* I reasoned. *"The baby has pointy feet."*

Then I learned this was not the baby kicking, after all. It was just a little gas, which meant that I was neither very thin, nor pleasant company. Maybe this is what they mean when they say the honeymoon is over. I'm fat and gassy, and Adam is stuck with me.

But at least he is going to be getting a free baby out of the deal. I hope that turns out to be a good thing, or it's going to be a long fifty years before I finally earn my gold watch. You do get a gold watch out of a successful marriage, right? I know my grandfather got one from the bank, and he didn't even have to sleep there. Staying married through thick and thin is surely more difficult. Especially this thick part.

The thicker I get, the more I think such things, even though Adam has been nothing short of wonderful about the hideous and earthy aspects of early pregnancy. Nonetheless, old insecurities and new neuroses are running pell-mell inside my head. They're shaking the floorboards like crazy, and I have to remind myself that it doesn't matter that I'm a little tubby. I'm making a baby. I've never been able to make a cake from scratch, and yet, I'm doing perfectly well here without even benefit of a recipe.

What really helped reassure me, though, was the baby, who kicked hard enough for me to feel when I was eighteen weeks along. The kick came right on schedule—a sign that even though I don't know what I'm doing here, even though I'm far from perfect, I'm doing something right. Adam and I were eating Thai food when I felt something strange, like a tiny ball bouncing in my stomach. It was firm and lively, like no gas pain I'd ever experienced. I soon realized what was happening. My eyes closed, and I felt my face go wide with the same smile I got when I found out I was pregnant.

For whatever reason, when I think about this baby, I can't help myself. I have to smile. I look like a Halloween pumpkin, all lit up, lumpy, and full of big, happy teeth. I'm a regular grinning machine. Unless, of course, this isn't really a smile after all, and it's just gas I'm feeling.

The Awful Truth about Pregnancy

Little did I know how hard it would be to keep up my strength during this ordeal. I am not one of the lucky people who glow during pregnancy, unless you count the glow of sweat I get after I throw up. I've been making progress on my pile of pregnancy books, so I was ready intellectually for a challenge. These books, I've found, are very good about telling you what symptoms you will face during the twenty-three or so months it takes to deliver a child. Okay. So it's not really twenty-three months, unless you're an elephant. But I digress.

In the end, they're like high school history readers describing the tortures General Washington's men faced during the snowy winter as they marched barefoot through Valley Forge. They can tell you about these things. But they don't really tell you what they're *like*. If they did, no one would get pregnant on purpose.

It starts with exhaustion. Before you even know you're pregnant, you will fall asleep on the couch at 7:30 P.M. And you won't even be aware that you're falling asleep. You'll just sit down, get comfortable, and then your husband will take a picture of you drooling. To create this feeling for yourself, take the kind of allergy pill that makes you sleepy and drink a beer.

And then there is the canine sense of smell. Every time someone opened the fridge, no matter where I was sitting, I could smell all the nasty stuff in there. To simulate this experience, mash up some garlic in a glass of orange juice. Toss in some meat, preferably ground and raw. Put your nose over the glass and inhale deeply. If your stomach rolls over, you now know how an ordinary icky smell turns into something deeply awful when you're under the influence of hormones.

There is also morning sickness. The books now cop to the fact that this can strike at any time of day, completely without warning. But you don't really know morning sickness until you've barfed in front of a crowd in a dangerous location. Next time you're in traffic, pull over really fast and stick your head out the door to upchuck without getting any on your clothes. The fear of being arrested for public vomiting only enriches the experience.

Your nose also will go into overdrive to produce snot. People will always think you have a cold. Let them. It's easier than explaining that hormones are making your mucus membranes hyperactive. No one really wants to hear that.

Likewise, weird things will happen to your hair. If you're like me, it will get sticky. Really sticky. Like you slept in a pan of honey. And you will think, *"Was I so tired last night I fell asleep in honey? It wasn't in the picture my husband took."* This is the time to buy expensive shampoo. For the first time in my life, I now use a more expensive hair product than the dog does.

And before you even show, you will get clumsy. Three times in one week, I spilled my lunch on my pants. The worst was teriyaki sauce. It looked like I had wet myself. Perhaps this is because you are so ravenously hungry, your eating gets a little frantic. This only gets more humbling when you are eating with coworkers who do not yet know you're expecting. To simulate the feeling, stand up. Rest your plate on one palm, and hold your fork in the hand you usually do not use for forking. Run. When you splash food across your clothes, you're there.

The maddening thing is, not everyone has the same symptoms. You can prepare yourself all you want, but you'll almost certainly have some new ones to add to the list. Or else, ordinary things take on a whole different meaning when you're expecting a child.

Nothing really prepares you for this. Five years ago, for example, I found a sugar-cube-sized tumor in my right breast. I was pretty scared; I'd already seen two young friends die of cancer. And the image of myself bald from chemotherapy, scarred from a mastectomy, was enough to make me weep. Not only was I stuck working in a lousy job, I also had a tumor. This wasn't the life I had signed up for, nor the life I expected when, as a child, I thought about the future. But statistics and fate were in my favor, and the lump turned out to be a benign tumor.

The day I had it removed, I went to a matinee, in celebration of my lively spirit. The thought of dying young was, of course, romantic. But I was happy that would not be my own ending. And the experience was one of the things that motivated me to make a better life for myself—to take a pay cut, move to a new city, and start over with the belief that I deserved a little joy. That risk paid off. I'm so much happier, so deeply in love, and so lucky in my work. I'm glad I suffered, just so I can appreciate this good life even more.

But I'm still a little haunted by the past. One night last month, as I massaged my sore, pregnant chest, I found a new lump—one that felt a little different from before. It scared me. Last week, I found myself lying on an examining room table in a dark, cold room with a bleak, scabby ceiling and a digital clock that flashed the wrong time in a steady rhythm, like a heartbeat.

Before I'd heard my child's heartbeat, I had things like matinees to live for. And the shallow truth is, dying young would have made a good story. No matter what, I'd have accomplished something worth talking about. But now I have seen my baby's tiny face on ultrasound. (I've seen her other end, too, so I know she's a girl.) She has my pointy chin. She has Adam's gangly legs. And so much more important than the story of my own life is hers. I don't want to miss it. Not one second.

I got some good news on the lump. Everything checked out just fine. But I'm learning now how my life will never be the same.

They tell you in books that you will love your child. They don't tell you how much you will want to live forever the first time you see your child's face—even if it is just a black-and-white ultrasound snapshot. There is no way to simulate this feeling, except maybe to imagine that all the love you've ever felt over your lifetime has transformed into a river, carrying you toward an inevitable destination. There's nothing like a new life inside of you to remind you of your own mortality and, suddenly, how much your life is worth.

Talking about Sex with Strangers

While there are many trials of pregnancy, there is one nice thing it does for you: It finally gets strangers to stop making small talk about the weather.

After all, why say, "Nice day out," when you can say, "When are you due? Will you pump your breasts at work? You're not actually drinking that toxic soda, are you?"

The reason people prefer talking about your unborn child

is that everyone knows you can't do anything about the weather—but you sure can do something about that baby.

There's something about pregnant women that really brings this trait out. This is understandable. Everyone wants babies to enter a perfect world in perfect health. But there is a limit to what a woman facing five months in a muumuu should have to tolerate. And if one more stranger passes along another piece of totally debatable wisdom, I'm going to retch. This morning sickness has to come in handy somehow.

For example, I've had people tell me that if I do not get an epidural block, I will probably die from twenty-seven hours of inhuman pain. And I've had people tell me that if I do get an epidural block, I am an incomplete woman. Probably a bad mother. And certainly an idiot. Beyond that, my uterus might split open.

My favorite advice, though, has to do with sex. The baby's, of course. I am temporarily uninterested in any other kind.

There are plenty of reasonable people who want to wait until the delivery to find out their child's sex because it's fun for them. Amen to that. But what's with the people who think finding out sooner is unnatural?

They look at you like you're one of those greedy kids who sneaks a peek at her Christmas presents. And even though I was a hardened peeker, I resent that. After all, I never got caught. And childbirth isn't Christmas, though I wouldn't mind if someone left me a plate of cookies as a thank-you for delivering.

Back in my prepregnancy days, I read that 71 percent of college-educated women accurately predicted the sex of their child. Since the odds were with me, I was completely sure I was going to have a boy from about the sixth week on—right when I started all that barfing. After all, what's more stomach-turning than a little boy, a little boy who would someday carry dead guppies in his back pockets? As a result, I thought a lot about boy names, whether I'd let him drive a car right away when he turned sixteen, and whether he'd go through a weird Oedipal phase because of breast feeding.

When I got an ultrasound at nineteen weeks, I merely glanced when the fetus generously offered up its little rump for close examination.

"Yep, oh yeah, that's a boy," I said. Adam and the ultrasound tech looked at me like I'd gone ape.

"It's a girl. There's nothing there," they both said.

Okay. So not only did I get more confirmation that I am in no way psychic, and possibly not qualified to be a wife, I was also surprised. Maybe even more surprised than I would have been had I waited for the delivery, because there would be no pain to divide my attention.

So I ask, why is it better not to know what you're having? Tradition? In that case, why not give birth in a one-room shack with a kettle full of boiling water that you brought into the house from the well using a bucket you made from a mighty oak tree you sawed down by hand? Right. I thought so.

On the other hand, there are many good reasons to find

out. Some genetic diseases, for example, are linked to a particular sex. Knowing about this beforehand is a great way for parents to prepare themselves for that particular challenge. More commonly, though, finding out the sex is the first major thing you know about the little person you're bringing into the world. And there's no such thing as knowing too much, too soon about your children. Until they're adults, that is, telling you that you're about to become a grandparent. Like one's parents, one's children should be virgins forever.

So I was wrong about having a boy. I adjusted my expectations, bought a couple pink outfits, and feel like I know my baby better already. And that's the best part of it all: slowly getting to know her. I've learned a few important things already. For example, I can't rest my arm on my stomach without being pummeled by at least eight tiny feet. This is not a child who will tolerate anyone cramping her style. And I have a feeling I know where this trait came from. If she actually does have eight feet, though, that's Adam's fault. He has extra ribs and teeth, though the latter were extracted in a series of traumatic visits to the dentist's office when Adam was in grade school.

Of course, there is always the possibility that I will be wrong about her puckish nature. After all, she's half Adam's child too. But in any case, I will be there to be wrong. And then we'll get on to the more important things in life.

Like where I'm going to hide the Christmas presents.

The Name Game

As a prospective parent, there's another thing besides all the sex questions that I dread. And that's the idea that yet another person will ask me, *"Hey. Have you picked a name yet?"*

Yes, I know there are more worthy things to fear—that my child will not be perfectly healthy, or that she will have blond hair and give my black-haired husband all sorts of crazy suspicions. But that's too much to think about, especially since I already have chronic heartburn.

I dread the name question largely because it's inevitable. Everyone asks it. Even the dog. I swear it; her favorite name so far is "Cookie?" She goes nuts when she hears it.

The problem with the name question is that there is no good answer. The person asking it has an agenda—much like the guy asking, "Did someone fart?" isn't looking for verification. He's looking for a confession and an apology. And even if it was the dog that tooted because she just ate another cookie, you're the one who smells like a liar.

And so it is with names. If you say you haven't picked one yet, people look at you funny, like you're going to be one of those freaks who calls the child "Hi, Baby" for the first two years of her life.

And because no one can stand the idea of a baby named Baby, they trot out their own lists. People mean well, I know. A baby's name has to last a lifetime. It's quintessential to her identity. And it's exciting to be part of that process. But there are three kinds of name-generators who like to torment pregnant women: the zealots, the proper noun enthusiasts, and the for-a-girl gang.

Zealots have serious yet arbitrary rules about your child's name. Back when I just knew the baby would be a boy, my brother-in-law Allan insisted that the child's name start with the letter A. This is because my husband is Adam, and Allan's son is named Andrew. It's a family tradition that goes back for two whole generations. Allan, who could get a duck excited about the opening day of hunting season, had the whole family looking for names. We'd get phone calls, instant messages, and e-mails, all filled with one wacky boy name after another. I'm sorry, but I just can't see raising a Li'l Abner.

Proper noun enthusiasts favor names of states, celebrities, and intangible concepts. Alabama, Earth—even Liberty. My father-in-law just met a Liberty. Apparently, she was stunning. He, therefore, thinks it would be a great name for his tenth grandchild. I guess when you already have a lot of grandkids, you can afford a novelty name. Either that, or he takes his job as a lawyer more seriously than I thought. In any case, I think I will be getting Mark some goldfish for Father's Day. He can name them Liberty, Justice, and For All, and I can continue my pursuit of happiness.

And then there's the for-a-girl gang. We've met many members, who just love saying, "What about [insert boy's name followed by dramatic pause] for a girl?" Pick a boy's name, any boy's name, Jeremy, Dave, Steve. No one ever says, "What about the name Priscilla—for a boy?"

This is nothing, though, compared to what happens when you've got a list of names you're considering. For every name on that list, people know someone who is either in jail, in rehab, or insane. My grandmother was Mary Ellen for the first few years of her life. But her parents changed her name to Eleanor when the other Mary Ellen in her small town went swimming in the deep end and never came back to shore. I don't know why my great-grandfather didn't also change his name at the same time. His name was Adolph, a name that is about as easy to pull off as Beelzebub or Genghis Khan.

Even my mom has gotten in on the fun. For a while, Natalie was on top of my list. I've always loved the name.

But not Mom. "Naaaaatalieeeeee," she said.

"What," I said. "You don't like it?"

"It's . . . okay."

My mother can pack a whole paragraph of meaning into a single word, just by the way she pronounces it. In this case, she was really saying: *"Don't even think of doing that. You may not have a room anymore that I can send you to, but I didn't raise you Catholic for nothing. Pack your emotional baggage; I'm booking you one-way tickets on a guilt trip, unless you stop that nonsense. Right this minute."*

Mom has taken to calling the baby Alice. Which is on the list. But it's not what my mother-in-law calls the baby. Carol calls her Lucy. Which is also on the list. And this terrifies me, since both of them repeatedly said, "It's your wedding," just a few years ago. Everyone who's married knows what that really means. I didn't think of registering disgruntledbride.com for nothing.

Meanwhile, Adam and I have come up with a great way to dodge the baby-name question. We just say there's a list, but that we won't pick a name until we see what she looks like. This doesn't mean we plan to get literal and call her Little Pink Alien. But it sure takes the pressure off, for another few months, anyway.

The Dad-to-Be's Chapter

I am the father-to-be, and this is (probably?) my one chapter. Which is fine, because that's what fathers-to-be usually get. One chapter.

I've discovered that if you pick up practically any guide to pregnancy, you will probably find a thin, solitary chapter, somewhere near the back of the book, entitled, "What *Dad* Can Do" or "Men: Be Involved" or "Get Off the Couch, You Jerk."

And I've found that this sole chapter will be filled with advice for men revolving around three common themes:

Stop watching sports and vacuum once in a while;

Yes, you and your one-track mind *can* have sex during pregnancy;

If you don't want to feel left out, why don't you join your wife and get some exercise too, fatty.

I'll tell you, these lonely chapters have served me well, and I'd like to recommend them to other fathers-to-be. They've been quite insightful, but not just because they've taught me how to pick a new car seat. They've also taught me a lot about other men.

In one guidebook, some author thought it necessary to write the words "You don't have to feel jealous that your wife is getting all the attention." Some other writer thought it would be a revelation to men that "If you're wife is tired, help out around the house a little."

And my favorite: Someone thought a man would really need to know that his wife "may like to find out that you find her more curvaceous shape attractive."

I can't help but wonder, *Who are the guys who need this advice?* What man sits there and steams about his wife getting attention? Who says, "I know you're tired, honey, but if you could just fix up the house a little"? What guy (anywhere, ever) is in any way subtle about his wife's curvaceous shape?

But here are respected Ph.D.s writing these words into practically every pregnancy book I see.

So now, I look around at other fathers and fathers-to-be and think to myself, huh, should I be watching more sports? Maybe I'm just a big wimp. But then I look at my wife—unconscious on the couch from chronic sleepiness even as I write this—and believe it or not, it really does occur to me that hey, *I* could put the laundry in the washer. And funny thing is, that occurred to me before she was pregnant, too.

So, let me take my one chapter and offer some manly advice that goes past the couch-potato themes:

Do not assemble the crib in the wrong room. It may be too wide for the door, and you're really going to be pissed off when you figure that out.

No matter how funny you think it is, do not joke about weight gain. It is never, ever, ever funny. That funny, that is.

What the baby wears home from the hospital matters. I dunno. Go figure.

If your wife wants lemonade at two-thirty in the morning, your first question should be "Country Time or Minute Maid?"

Photos are okay, but not spontaneous photos. Video cameras are off limits.

Maintain following distance, wear your seat belt, don't change lanes too quickly, and put away the cell phone. The world needs you.

If you think you're ready to view a live childbirth, you're not. Think again. Go rent a video from the public library, and *do not* let your wife's birth be your initiation. Whoever said childbirth was "beautiful" took a few too many fertility pills, if you know what I mean.

Finally, I have this piece of advice for women and the writers of pregnancy books.

Women have many milestones during pregnancy. From the first signs of morning sickness, to crossing trimesters, to feeling that first kick and then another, and another. But there really is only one real rite of passage for men during pregnancy, and at least all the fathers I've talked to confirm this with me.

It's the moment—some moment—when it really sinks in.

It'll be buying baby clothes for the first time, or hearing the heartbeat, or putting the new sheets in the crib that does it. Doesn't matter. But *something* will do it.

Something at some point is going to say to Dad, "This is really happening." And when that happens, he'll get a lump in his throat, he'll probably shut up for a minute, and if he's like me, he'll wonder whether anything else in the world has ever really mattered.

That's the thing for which there is no preparation, and it will be the one time during pregnancy when the father-to-be looks at the mother-to-be and thinks, I need you for this.

Finally! Some Good Advice

Every Thursday for the last couple years, I've eaten lunch with a grade-schooler named Mark. We chow down cheeseburgers and little mummified Tater Tots, and we play games, invent stories, and sometimes make origami water balloons.

Over the years, I've given Mark plenty of advice. "Remember, when you're folding origami, be very careful to match up the corners or your balloon won't be *perfect*." And the classic:

"Mark, you will break that plastic flamingo if you keep slamming its head like that. And then we won't be able to use it to pick up worms."

Poor Mark. He did nothing to deserve this kind of advice. But he got his turn when I told him that my stomach wasn't just getting big from the cafeteria food.

"Congratulations!" he said. "I have some advice for you."

"Advice?" I thought. *"From a nine-year-old? And from one who is a little hard on the flamingos?"*

"Don't let your kids run wild," he said. "People will have more respect for you, and will like your kids better, if they behave in public."

I couldn't believe this was the sliver of wisdom a nine-year-old boy chose to give. Not only was it pithy and direct, it made a lot of sense. Most important, it wasn't selfish or scheming. It was useful, and I've added it to an ever-expanding file of actually useful pregnancy and parenting advice. Here are some more favorites:

On morning sickness

During the Ed Debarfic's incident, I was paranoid about getting dehydrated and drying up my walnut-sized baby, so I kept downing huge glasses of red Gatorade every time I thought I could take it. And of course, I would puke it right back up.

I called my doctor dad back home. He said, "What'd you go and do that for? Your stomach's just a bag. You can't just fill it like that."

As I used to want to do in childhood, I called my real doctor for a second opinion. She said pretty much the same thing, only a lot more nicely. "Nibble on a saltine and then wait an hour, and have just a few sips of fluid."

It worked.

On child care

A couple friends with babies have said that even when I'm home, I should find a good baby-sitter every once in a while, so I can take a break and do whatever it is I need to do to stay sane and happy. And once I figure out what *that* is, I'll be set.

Also, friends and family have said the best time for Adam to take time off work is when the baby is a few months old. Everyone else will have lost interest, I'll be exhausted, and the baby will be alert enough to be interesting to Adam. Maybe not as interesting as a computer video game. But I can be optimistic here.

On labor and delivery

Another friend recommends staying home as long as possible after labor starts so that I can stay relaxed (and avoid getting shoved into a teeny room when all the so-called "birthing suites" are full). Of course, my mom, who nearly gave birth to me in an elevator because her labor was only forty minutes, thinks I should go to the hospital right away.

I think they're both right.

Another experienced Dad said to be ready for anything in the delivery room. His wife was planning on natural childbirth. A ruptured placenta meant a ninety-second C-section, which my friend missed because he was busy putting on scrubs.

On names

A friend, crediting the late Erma Bombeck, passed this one along. Before you settle on a name, stand at your front door and holler it for fifteen minutes. Have your husband do the same. Apparently, that's how long it takes a kid to come to dinner. This one might get us in trouble with our condo association. But I'm going to do it anyway. This crazy behavior will only help Adam and me fit in better with our neighbors, who have a lot of quirks of their own.

On making the baby bleed

This is my favorite. Apparently, newborns have dragon fingernails that do harm to all they contact. But if you cut these claws, they might bleed—so that the whole world, especially the pediatrician, will know you're an unfit mother. I am certain I would have drawn blood had not two friends with infants let me know that a nail file is the right tool for the job.

I can't imagine a worse feeling than knowing I caused my child's first worldly pain. As parent-to-be, I think a lot about the things that hurt me as a child—both inside and out. And I think about how I can spare my child the pains I went through. That's one of the pledges I would guess all parents make: to give their children a smoother ride than they got growing up.

And that's why people give advice. Because growing up is so very hard. From bloody fingertips to bruised knees to the painful metamorphosis of soul that is adolescence, childhood is packed with experiences that can damage or build strength.

Good parents are the ones who know how—and when—to advise. Even when their kids are grown up and barfing Gatorade while their bodies quietly manufacture children of their own.

That's the thing with advice. The good stuff is good because it comes with love. The other stuff, well, those people probably just let their kids run wild anyway. And I know what Mark would have to say about that.

Maternity-Clothes-Minded

If you do feel like behaving badly, pregnancy is a great time to be smug and superior. In fact, it's one of the only times in your life you ever stand a chance of getting away with it.

There are several reasons for this: Once people know you're pregnant, people give you a wide berth—before you're actually wide enough to need it. Why is this? I'm not sure. It could be the modern office-dweller's fear of hormones and other organic phenomena, or it could be because your cubicle is no longer stacked with empty Diet Coke cans and Cheetos bags, and you suddenly look respectable.

Whatever the reason, people cut pregnant women a lot of slack. And while I'm not complaining about it, it does have its drawbacks. When you're getting the special treatment, for example, you're much more likely to make grand pronouncements about what you will—and will not—do. This is a dangerous thing.

As usual, I learned way too late to be very careful about this. For example, I said to many, many people that I would *never* wear those hideous maternity clothes.

Part of this stems from the horror I experienced on my first maternity-clothes-shopping trip. I went with a friend who's a couple months farther along than I am. Our first stop was a store stocked with floppy, bow-necked floral-print dresses, aggressively cheerful T-shirts, and a major display of disturbingly large maternity underpants and nursing bras. The store's virtue was that it was cheap. But when I saw my dear friend buy a pair of the giant hipsters because she had developed a pregnancy rash called "pups," I nearly died.

Scarred from this experience, I went to a faraway outlet mall and bought some very large yet still fashionable men's jeans. I was going to go through this pregnancy looking like me, just a little bigger and a little more mannish. I allowed myself an extra six to ten inches in the waist in each pair. At the time, not a one of them stayed up unless I bunched up the waistband and held it tight.

Leap ahead in time a few months. Even though I am now nearly seven months pregnant, and have the belly for it, they still won't stay up. And this time, there's no extra fabric to grab. When I wear these pants, they slowly migrate during the day from my middle to just below my watermelon-sized stomach. If there were a sound effect that accompanied this, it would be the whiny, farty, dying sound a balloon makes when you slowly release its air.

When I wear my Giant Man Pants, I look funny from the front and side. And if I had the courage to look at my rear in a mirror, I would know for sure how I looked from the back. As it is, I do have the imagination to guess.

Back before I had experienced the trauma of sinking pants, I would have said I looked like a plumber from behind. Now, I know better than to make fun of plumbers and other people who, as they say, "crack a smile."

The pregnant belly is a rather firm mass. Unlike what I expected, it's not a squishy, malleable animal that can be molded to the fashion tastes of its owner. The thing is as hard as a baked ham, and about the same size, but without the lovely glaze or delicious smell. Try dressing a ham in little blue jeans and taking it out for a walk, and you'll suddenly develop a lot more compassion for plumbers and all other men with drum-tight potbellies wearing saggy pants. Why? Because men still can't buy everyday clothes with Spandex in them. But pregnant women can. And probably should.

After I got to the point where I needed the Giant Man

Pants, but didn't fill them out, my sisters performed a fashion intervention. We went to a slightly more upscale store than the House of Jurassic Panties, and I bought some overalls, some Capri pants, and a couple of shirts. My mom sewed me three more maternity tops, one of which I have already outgrown. I bought a few things online, though I resisted the $400 leather pants being hyped online by a supermodel-turned-supermom.

And then my mother-in-law came for a visit, took a good look at me, and went to the fanciest maternity store in town and bought one of everything, which I had to exchange for a larger size. I am still depressed. Every day is a bad thigh day when you're pregnant.

I know I'm not the only one who lives in a fantasy world when it comes to the imagination vs. the reality of pregnancy. In fact, I've encountered such crazy thoughts, even on very reputable Web sites. One blithely suggested that I "might want to get a maternity swimsuit" once I hit the third trimester. I *might* want to? Yes. Just like the grocery store courtesy clerk who wisely chooses a large, reinforced sack instead of a sandwich baggie when packing a twenty-pound turkey, pregnant women *must* wear maternity bathing suits into the pool. And this is well before the third trimester ticks around.

So, here I sit, huge and humbled. There is one bright side to this, though. My mother-in-law still thinks I'm a small.

Chapter 4

The Third Trimester

If pregnancy were a book they would cut the last two chapters.
—Nora Ephron

That is so true. But since you paid for this, you might as well keep reading.

Where Babies Come From

Now that I'm waddling down the pregnancy homestretch, I finally know where babies come from. I knew the mechanical part already, of course. As part of her job, my mom teaches sex ed, and unfortunately, this is the kind of conversation our family often has around the dinner table. When I add that my dad was a surgeon, I'll let you figure out the other kinds of conversations that we regularly have. It's a wonder any of us can still eat meat.

The closer I get to my due date, the more I obsess over women who have small children. I was in the hardware store last week when I saw a serene blond lift her rowdy little boy out of the shopping cart. And all I could think was, "She did it. That child was in her. He came out of her. And she's smiling."

Of course, the rowdy little boy was about three years old. What I wanted to ask the woman, but didn't—as I know what kind of public behavior looks like insanity—was, how long did it take? How long did it take before you finally felt like a mother?

Two weeks ago, a few days after my friend Elaine had her baby (following a quick and painless twenty-six-hour labor), I got to hold little Morgan, a gorgeous creature with wide eyes and dark, dark hair. My arm practically fell asleep under the mass of this perfect infant. Everyone says newborns are unbelievably tiny. This is a myth perpetuated by people who aren't carrying babies, or facing the pain of childbirth anytime soon.

No one ever says, "Hey. That McDonald's quarter-pounder sure looks like a tiny meal!" And no one toting a freshly eaten quarter-pounder in his stomach thinks, "What a tiny little snack I've just consumed." Imagine giving birth to thirty-six quarter-pounders, all bundled into one hyperkinetic Happy Meal, and you start to realize that newborns are anything but small.

And this particular one was huge. At nine pounds, she was larger than average. And I kept looking from the baby to Elaine thinking, *"My God. This giant baby was inside you two days ago. And now, here she is."*

The closer I get to motherhood, the more the women who've had children become heroes to me—and the more ridiculous I find the prediction that someday women won't need men to make babies. While it's true that women do the heavy lifting on this job, I can't imagine wanting to have a child without a partner. I know, I know. Lots of people do it solo. And lots of women, particularly those of my generation, feel good about saying, "If I don't find the right man, I will raise a child on my own."

This is one of those things that seem matter-of-fact. Courageous. Independent. And a whole lot easier said than done. Some people are able to pull this off, and I think that's great. But it's not a choice I would ever make, knowing what I now know about just the beginning of the process.

Adam and I spend an awful lot of time with each other. By some estimates, almost twenty-four hours a day. That much time together would kill a lot of couples, but I can't imagine living our life any other way. Sure, it's convenient that he makes me frozen lemonade when I'm hot and my hands are so bloated I can barely grip a glass. And it's sweet when he brings me Tums at 2 A.M. because I'm having a heart attack. (Okay, it's heartburn. But it feels like a heart attack.) He sometimes even rolls up the cuffs of my giant jeans, because I can't bend over so well anymore. But it's not the errand service that I need so much. It's his company and the knowledge that we're each other's strength from now on, a bond sealed in the creation of a child.

Newborns are enormous in more ways than one. Giving birth is just a small part of giving life. And that's the biggest thing anyone could possibly contemplate. It's so big that Adam and I have never really even talked about it—though we've certainly had the time. We have a really long commute, and our car stereo got stolen last year, which means we actually have to converse.

And I don't think it's because we're in denial. It's just one of those things that is too large to pin down with mere words. There's no conversation that could sum up the meaning and importance of life. The meaning of life is in the living, the everyday choices and events that end up in either happiness or despair. You don't talk about it. You just do it.

A new life, whether a six-pounder or a nine-pounder, is too large to entrust to one person alone. Not just for the baby, but for the parent. Even for two parents.

Babies may come from just two individuals. But to survive in this world—and to find a place—people need a lot more than that. In a few weeks, when this baby is born, Adam and I will say she's our baby. But really, she will belong to the world, to the kind people and the cruel alike. Her fate will be a combination of the choices we make, the choices she makes, and the choices that others around her make, with a bit of luck thrown in for utter unpredictability.

I guess this is what makes babies seem so tiny to people— the knowledge that they're utterly dependent on us. It's wishful thinking for parents to believe they can provide everything their children need to have lives made from the stuff of dreams. Life is so much harder than that.

No, babies are tiny because their lives depend on the world. And that never changes, even when we're all grown up.

Everything a Baby Really Needs

The more pregnant I get, the more I think about genetics. Last night, for instance, I had a dream that I was not, in fact, carrying a human child. As the demons that came to the door informed me, I was going to give birth to a monster. And instead of having the baby at the hospital like I've planned, they were going to snatch her the old-fashioned, demon way—through my stomach. This, apparently, was to spare me the public humiliation of raising an actual devil-child.

I have since made a note to check Adam's family tree for possible evil lineage. His family seems really wonderful, but can a person be too careful about this? My dad assures me our family is clean. Which is not to say that we don't have our own genetic quirks.

Some, we come by honestly. My grandfather, for example, was a thrifty, resourceful man. He had to be, because his family didn't have any money. He once drew stripes on a plywood floor to make it look like tongue-and-groove hardwood. My mother, who absolutely cannot say "no" to a free sample, still talks about how wonderful the floor looked. And I believed her. Until I really thought about it just now.

My parents have continued the tradition of thrift by holding on to their twenty-seven-year-old shag carpet in the living room. The dogs use it as their own personal towel when they're wet. I am the third-generation cheapskate. My sister Susan used to refuse to come over to my house unless I turned the heat on. For me, 58 degrees was no problem. If you can see your breath, you know you're alive. But I do recall one New Year's Eve where the whole family sat on the folding chairs in my living room, shivering glumly. And I don't think it was just the crunchy lasagna I had served them.

Like other things with pregnancy, though, you overcome many of your natural tendencies for the sake of your unborn child. I no longer drink coffee, and I used to be one of those people who could postpone going to work for an hour by nursing a mug.

The biggest change pregnancy has meant is that I've spent a lot more money, both on clothes for me and stuff for the baby. Together, Adam and I have bought a car seat, a crib, a changing table, and a bassinet (because he put the crib together in the wrong room and we decided to spend $50 instead of reassembling). We've bought thumb-sized red sneakers. Cute little outfits with dog paws, bunnies, and peas on them. A star-shaped paper lamp. And lots and lots of cotton sleepers.

Some of these things, of course, you find on the lists of

baby essentials that are all over the Internet and inside those warehouse-sized baby emporiums. I take most of these lists with a giant grain of salt, because they claim things not found in nature—like baby monitors—as essentials. I may be hepped up on hormones, but there's no way anyone can convince me a baby monitor is an essential. Nice to have, yes. But essential? When were these invented—1980? Sure seems like a lot of babies lived without them. Adam likes them because they're like walkie-talkies. But that's a different matter, entirely.

My very wise doctor told me that all I really needed for the baby was a few T-shirts and some diapers. What she was really saying is that babies' needs are pretty simple at first. Just food, warmth, clean bottoms, and love. But first-time parents—and probably all parents—are saying something else every time they crack open their wallets. There's a reason money says, "In God We Trust." It's our way of saying, "God help us. We're having a baby, and we're don't know if we're equipped."

The easy way to feel ready, of course, is to fill your home with stuff. Little plastic snot-removal balls, Q-tips, rubbing alcohol, twenty-eight books on parenting, five kinds of prenatal vitamins, mentally stimulating mobiles and sponge bathtubs with plastic duckies that turn white when the water gets too hot. Adam and I even bought a new car—a statement that our tiny purple beater with the cracked windshield and stolen stereo just didn't make us feel like good parents.

It Could Happen to You

Kind friends who've gone through this before often have good, practical advice—not to mention hand-me-downs that help stem the cash hemorrhage. One couple, for example, just lent us a little bouncy chair. Adam and I were lukewarm on it until they said, "Olivia spent three or four hours a day in it."

That was enough to make both of us reach for the chair—and I don't bend over for much these days.

I think I'm just about done with the preinfant shopping. After the baby is born and I've had her for a while, I'll probably know which purchases were smart and which could have waited. But I'm beginning to suspect that the feeling of "What if I'm inadequate? What if I don't provide everything she needs to be a good, loving person?" is the essence of parenthood. Wisdom, of course, is knowing the difference between what you have to buy and what you have inside of you to give. I'm still in the phase where I think a pink tankini is a good idea for a newborn. Something tells me I have a ways to go.

Womb with a View

Now that I'm having a baby, some of the crazy things my mom said are finally starting to make some sense. She used to tell us, for example, that there was such a thing as Too Much Fun. This would happen most often when we were in high school, on those rare occasions when we planned to go out for fun on both Friday and Saturday nights. She had a certain way of saying it. Her voice got a little low and she drew out each word—kind of like a Gregorian chant.

"You've had Toooo Muhhhcch Fuhhhhnnn."

We called it "exceeding the fun quotient." And we all still tease her today for saying that. Even my work-loving dad teases her, and he hasn't so much as seen a movie in a theater since *Parenthood*. My parents saw it together in 1989, when they had five teenagers to deal with. Looking back, I'm wondering if they thought it was going to be a helpful documentary.

The closer I get to my due date, the more my mom's irrational side makes sense. I'm becoming a little insane myself. It could be the heat. It could be the incredible pressure the baby's little bottom is putting on my rib cage. I think I know how a walnut must feel when it's getting cracked open. Those poor walnuts, so round, so innocent, so covered in stretch marks. Anyway, I'm starting to think irrational behavior is just one of those side effects of motherhood.

For me, it all went downhill about three months ago, when I had my first ultrasound. It was a miserable day. I had a disgusting cold. Disgusting colds are different from the garden-variety ones. Unfortunately, they're the only kind you have when you're pregnant and your hormones are helping you produce rivers and rivers of snot. In addition to that, I was coughing like someone who really wanted to shed a lung. And to prepare for the exam, I also drank four glasses of water an hour before the examination was to begin.

I showed up fifteen minutes before my appointment time, just like they asked. I was feeling a little antsy. Not only was I about to see my baby for the first time, I was also the equivalent of a human water balloon. But Adam was with me. And he helped those fifteen minutes pass quickly. Unfortunately, the next hour of waiting went a lot more slowly. And the totally unfeeling woman behind the hospital counter didn't help.

"If you have to go to the bathroom, just go," she said, obviously not caring that I would have had to gulp more water and wait until my bladder was full again in order to get a good look at the baby.

"There are sometimes emergencies that cause delays," she said, when I asked what was causing the holdup.

And I was thinking, *Does a human being exploding in your waiting room from the sheer pressure of her bodily fluids count as an emergency? Because that can be arranged.*

I managed to keep it together using my patented "mind over bladder" technique, which once kept me from peeing for three days and two nights on a winter camping trip. I didn't want to leave a yellow hole in the snow for all my sixth-grade classmates to see. After what felt like another three days and two nights, they took us back to the exam room. I climbed on the table, the tech greased up my stomach, and there it was: the baby's head.

"Brain, brain," I thought. *"Where's the brain?"*

"And there's the brain," the tech said.

I was so relieved. This feeling only grew when she passed the probe over my stomach, revealing the tiny hands, the tiny feet, and the tiny, beating heart within me. A complete person, very small, who from this first look, appeared perfectly healthy, normal, and comfortable.

The only bad part at all was that when I coughed, which was about every five seconds, she looked pretty miserable in there. She even covered her head with her arms, in the classic "Not in the head!" position I mastered as a soccer player. Seeing your tiny baby flail, even if she is perfect, does not make a person feel like a good mother. And I have it captured on videotape, so that I can feel guilty frequently and conveniently, and for the rest of my life.

Guilt aside, the experience was an amazing thing, a miracle really. And also the beginning of the end for my sanity. Since then my sister, who is an ultrasound technologist, has given me a second peek, just to see. And the baby still looks great. I, on the other hand, am a mess. I have regular dreams that something is wrong, usually my fault. Last night, I dreamed that I slept through her birth and then put her in the washing machine. I often fear that once she's born, I'll drop her. Or yank off her umbilical stump. Or I won't know how to help her stop crying. Or I'll give her bad career advice.

Children, of course, are resilient. So are parents. My mom and I have forgiven each other for all the little mistakes we made in the name of love or, in my case, adolescence. For Mom, the fun quotient was her way of saying, "I'm not crazy about you kids driving around late at night in that van. Stay home. Study. That will get you into a better college, anyway." For me, the sight of my child—this miracle I do not deserve— is a symbol that the world has trusted me with more joy, and more responsibility, than a person could imagine. For the first time in my life, I actually feel as though I have exceeded the fun quotient. There's no going back, only the countdown of days until my life is no longer my own.

And as I get closer and closer to it, I am beginning to understand what makes parents so crazy: the desire to keep these children as perfect as the day they're born, the challenge of giving roots to an angel and wings to a tree.

On Childbirth and Cheese-Steak

The closer I get to my due date, the more I think of the act of childbirth. This fills me with much the same feeling of calm I would get by gazing into the eyes of an irritated rhino. The first time I saw a baby being born, I was a seventh-grade sex-ed student. At the time, I figured, hey, I read Judy Blume's books, what else do I need to know? Can I please be excused?

Fat chance. Kids do not get to read their way out of sex ed. Especially if they are the daughters of nurses who still correct you if you say, "Man, my stomach is full of baby." (Yes, Mom. It's a uterus. Uterus, uterus, uterus. And it's still full of baby.)

So, just before lunch, the teachers herded our class into the choir room, sat us on the risers, turned off the lights, and popped in the film. As with all childbirth films, this one started up with an earnest hippie couple talking about the miracle of pregnancy. And then it cut to the birth, which didn't look particularly miraculous to my twelve-year-old eyes. Rather, it looked squirty and gross. After a few heavily edited minutes, the baby came out and her mother named her "Meeghan, my beautiful Meeghan."

At that moment, the name Meeghan came right off my list forever. Totally irrational, I know. Meeghan is a very nice name, but for someone else's baby. The movie ended, and we all went solemnly to the cafeteria for lunch. A very quiet lunch, and no one would eat their Italian olives because some smarty-pants called them placentas.

In retrospect, this *had* to be more than just a sex-ed video. Ronald Reagan was in office, after all. I think it was part of the larger "Scared Celibate" program meant to keep the nation's youth chaste and possibly thin, if they make a practice out of showing childbirth before lunch.

Since becoming pregnant, I've seen three more babies born on videotape in a childbirth education class meant for expectant couples. The experience wasn't nearly so bad as the first go-around. That means either the videos we see as kids are much scarier, or I've grown up. The childbirth instructor said she thought it was the former. But more likely, it's probably because Adam and I got the serious giggles when one of the subjects said to his obviously struggling and nauseous wife,

"I'll bet you're regretting that cheese-steak sub right about now."

I don't know what was funnier—that a husband would actually say that, or that a woman in labor would think, *"Something meaty and cheesy will really power me through these contractions."*

Perhaps more intimidating was one of the other women in the video, who serenely breathed through her labor pains and got to be six centimeters dilated before she even went to the hospital. She had quiet and loving conversations with her husband. She sat in a rocking chair like a queen. And she struggled no more than as if she was gathering wildflowers from a field behind her cottage.

Steak, cheese, and inhuman serenity aside, the class was really helpful—in different ways for me than for Adam.

I've read quite a few books and theories about the "best" way to give birth. Adam, on the other hand, lost the book I bought him, and instead has spent most of his discretionary childhood education time taking care of my bizarre requests and talking to his sisters, who have had seven children between them. To his credit, he did read the eighteen-page pamphlet we got from the pediatrician. But he got hung up on the sentence that read, "Burp baby between breasts."

"Between your breasts?" he said. "I thought you did it over your shoulder."

I had to explain to him that babies nurse from one side at a time, and that the burp was like a little break. A commercial between TV shows. A palate cleanser following the main course. A seventh-inning stretch. This is why women—not men—nurse children. We aren't quite so literal. Especially about breasts.

Anyway, Adam said the biology and the coping tips were helpful. Especially because the instructor was careful to point out that there's a whole list of ways to cope with the pain, and that some would work, while others might not, and that we were free to choose. This means we won't have to do that goofy breathing unless it's actually helpful.

This is something I had already gathered from reading, but it was nice to have an experienced teacher reaffirm it. Though a lot of books insist their one method is the best, any reasonable person is going to conclude that there's probably a bit of truth in all of them. And that it's a parent's job to choose.

This is the true benefit of childbirth education—not to find the right way to have a baby, but to find your way. And to be courageous about it, because there are a lot of busybodies in the world who will tell you that you're wrong, and that you'll have a terrible experience if you don't change your mind.

As different as the videos made childbirth appear, one thing happened that didn't happen to me in seventh grade. I had to fight back tears each time the parents held their baby for the first time. To my surprise, I wasn't the only one.

"I'm going to cry when she's born," Adam told me after class. "I won't be able to help myself."

And neither will I. I will weep with relief, with exhaustion, and with undiluted joy.

I don't know how long the delivery will take. I don't know what the contractions will feel like. I don't know if I'll have an epidural block or not. I don't know which coping techniques will work. And I really don't care.

The one thing I do know is that I will not utter the words, "Honey. It's time. And let's get a Happy Meal on the way."

There's only so much happiness a person can take, you know. And I think seeing a brand-new baby—especially your own—is pretty much the limit.

The Secret Fantasy of All Pregnant Women

As much as we look forward to the moment when labor is over and we're holding our babies, pregnant women are an otherwise diverse lot.

You've got your Earth Mothers, who think of pregnancy as the organic equivalent of Woodstock. It's a huge celebration, meant to be wallowed in publicly. And possibly without clothing, and ideally, in lots of mud.

There are the Saintly Ladies. For them, peopling the Earth is something to bear quietly from behind a high-necked floral dress. They never complain. Their cheeks just occasionally get rosy. And they look annoyingly beautiful.

There are the Power Mothers, who would just as soon gestate their babies in Mason jars. They're busy, after all. They add extra pages to their calfskin appointment books just to accommodate the C-section appointment, scheduled just before that big trade show in NewYorkParisMilan.

And there are the Martians, who find every second of pregnancy to be pure and utter pleasure. They especially love broadcasting their message to the regular women who puke, weep, waddle, worry, and get half their calories from Tums. "Gosh, I don't know what you're complaining about," they say. "I just *love* being pregnant."

No matter how a woman feels *about* being pregnant—and no matter how she feels *being* pregnant—I have come to believe that we all share a fantasy. And it's not that the fathers of our children will suddenly get great at foot massages.

Rather, it's the glorious dream that the baby will come early.

Not too early, of course. Premature birth is a serious problem. Many women have heroically braved months of bed rest without going homicidal. Others—the ones who sit by incubators reading and singing to their tiny, tiny infants—are even more amazing with their patience, their courage, and their hope.

What I'm talking about is a lot more petty and selfish. It's the fantasy that the baby will come just early enough—maybe a week or two.

There are many reasons women have this dream, not the least of which has to do with the size of the baby's head. The difference between a six-pound baby and an eight-pound baby isn't really two pounds. It's the half inch of cranial diameter.

It's also alarming, in your last few weeks, how large your

abdomen gets. When I sit now, mine folds regally over the top of my thighs, keeping them nice and warm. Meanwhile, the top of my own personal incubator is so high that I occasionally lose sensation in the skin up there, and have to pinch and slap it to make it come back to life. If I sit for too long, I get what I call "crazy leg"—it's the irrepressible urge to kick something really hard.

Just getting out of bed turns into a daily drama, a little like Kafka's *Metamorphosis*. Like a cockroach that's been flipped onto its back, I have to rock back and forth several times to build the momentum I need to right myself. The only difference between me and Kafka's monstrous vermin is that cockroaches don't grunt.

At times like this, I wonder how much my skin can stretch without bursting. Especially when the baby moves, because her little protruding body parts make my stomach look like a pan of Jiffy Pop.

I think to myself, *"It's the middle of summer. I'm hot, I'm numb, I'm being inflated in freakish ways I can't predict or control. And I still have a few weeks to go!"*

In addition to this, there's also the very important consideration of the adorable little clothes you've acquired. The sooner the baby comes, the sooner you get to see what she looks like wearing them.

Finally, just the thought of seeing your child after months and months of anticipation is a thrill.

Because I am a realistic optimist—the kind who hopes for

the best and prepares for the worst—I have been expecting to go past my due date. I guessed a week late, in fact, when I put my dollar into the baby pool. The way I figured, if I was going to be playing the extended dance mix of pregnancy, I might as well win $20.

But then something surprising happened. At my checkup, my doctor got a slightly startled look and said the baby was engaged and it looked as though I'd been having some contractions.

"Better cut back on the swimming workouts," she said. "We don't want you to have the baby yet."

I really, really didn't expect to hear anything like this. I had a lot of loose ends to tie up at work. I hadn't washed the onesies. I hadn't even bought diapers. And my swimming workouts hadn't been *that* strenuous. It's true that I hadn't been paddling merrily along. I swam fast. I did flip turns. I wanted those people who stared at me in my giant black-and-white maternity suit to think, "Hey. Free Willy's got moves," when they saw me take to the lanes. Also, the exercise felt great.

But I followed orders. I also washed baby clothes, bought diapers, and called Adam, ostensibly to update him on the news, but really just to scare him a little. That will never stop being fun for me.

Now, three weeks later, the doctor says I look just fine. In fact, the baby is riding higher, and I don't look in any way like someone who'll be giving birth immediately. At first, this was unhappy news. I was kind of looking forward to shrinking back to normal size. In this heat, my fingers turn into sausages if I so much as look at a pickle. I would like my hands back, please.

The closer I get to the due date, I realize that having the baby may shrink my fingers and make it easier to type. But I will not be getting my hands back. In fact, they will be busy doing the most important work they've ever done—tending a new life, and over the course of many years, guiding her gently into adulthood.

Forty weeks is a long time to be pregnant. But it's not a long time to prepare for the work of parenthood. So I've stopped fantasizing about having this baby early. She can take all the time she wants. I'm going to need it.

Letters to a Baby on the Way

I turn thirty tomorrow, and I don't care. I know, I know. It's supposed to be one of life's milestones. In my grandmother's era, it was considered to be the start of middle age. My mom tells the story of when Greema returned to work after having her first two children. She was in her mid-thirties and wanted to know, "Do you hire older women?"

When I was a kid, I used to wonder what I'd be doing on my thirtieth birthday—and how glamorous I would be. I had a similar daydream about New Year's Eve 1999. Would I be wearing a little black dress? Sipping champagne with someone mysterious in an exotic spot? As it turned out, I ushered in the new millennium at home with family and friends, wearing a turtleneck. They drank the champagne; I had sparkling cider. While everyone who could went out on the roof of the condo to watch fireworks, Adam, my grandmother, and I held hands on the couch and watched the party on TV.

On my birthday, all I really want is a cool day and permission to go barefoot. This means someone will have to cut my toenails because I can no longer reach them and breathe at the same time.

Either I've turned into a total loser, or there's something about being ten days from your due date that makes other things feel way, way more important than watching your age clock flip a decade. By other things, I mean finding a comfortable chair and enjoying all-you-can-eat ice cubes from the freezer.

I still love birthdays, of course. But other people's, I'm discovering, are a lot more interesting. Particularly the one coming any day now.

I'm pretty sure this will be my daughter's worst birthday ever. No one ever talks about how bad childbirth is for babies. Everyone is way too preoccupied with how much pain childbirth is for the mother. I know I am. But newborns get the worst end of the deal by far. Can you imagine the headaches they must have? Yes, I know their skulls change shape to make birth possible. But who says this doesn't *kill?* And there's no such thing as a cranial block.

With that in mind, I've decided I want every birthday after this one to get my daughter one step closer to the happy, safe environment of the womb. I want her to have perfect happiness, but this time, without all that amniotic fluid making her wrinkly.

So, I've compiled advice I wish I had at each of my milestone birthdays.

On your first birthday

Dear baby,

Candles are hot. Blow yours out before you grab a chunk of cake.

Love,
Mom

On your fifth birthday

Dear daughter,

I hope you are having a better fifth birthday party than I had. On mine, we went out on a boat and the police stopped us to squeeze our life preservers. My sister's had a hole in it. It took the cops forever to finish. The kids who were back on the shore were furious, because they thought we got a longer boat ride. While we did, in fact, spend more time on the boat, we only went about a hundred yards. So everyone except the police officers was thoroughly miserable.

The point is, life is often unfair—whether you're a parent or a kid, and even people who look like they have everything sometimes aren't having the greatest time. I'll do my best to make sure your life preserver has no holes.

Also, now that you're getting ready for kindergarten, you need to know a couple of things. I know I've said before that nose picking is a bad idea. It's a really bad idea once you're in school. Also, if you have to go to the bathroom, just ask. And remember to flush and wash your hands.

Love,

Mom

On your thirteenth birthday

Dear daughter,

Today, someone will tell you that you're now a teeny-bopper. Yes, this annoyed me too. Just be polite.

I have some good news for you, and I have some bad news. The good news is, you're in for a lot of fun. You can see movies with some rough language and "situations." You can go on hikes at school. You can stay home without a baby-sitter and talk on the phone until your ear turns red.

The bad news is you will make some haircut decisions that will plague you for the rest of your life. Some of these decisions may also diminish the fun you would have had today if you had just listened to me.

But this is where you start getting your independence, and from now on, you can do whatever you want with your hair.

Also, your father wants you to know that he's sorry about the braces. Bad teeth came from his side of the family.

Love,
Mom

On your eighteenth birthday

Dear daughter,

This has been such a big year for you. You graduated from high school, and are getting ready to head off to college. This is the year people will say, "You're an adult now."

Ignore them. They're just saying that because they can't think of anything else to talk about. Turning eighteen doesn't mean that suddenly, you're losing the freedom of childhood and entering the indentured servitude of adulthood.

You've spent your whole life becoming an adult— which basically means taking responsibility for your actions and your own well-being. Remember learning to flush? That was one of the first ways you took care of your own messes.

Adulthood is not a loss of childhood. That's because childhood is generally vastly overrated. Not everyone achieves adulthood, by the way, no matter how old they get.

Very often, these are the people for whom high school was the high point of their lives. These are the people who are popular just because they're good-looking, or they drive the right cars—not because of who they are, what they have going on inside their heads, and how they treat other people. And I mean all other people, not just the ones who can give them something.

Celebrate being eighteen. It means you can vote, which is one small step toward influencing your future. And I say influencing on purpose. There is no controlling the future—only shaping it by your everyday actions and the people you choose to spend time with.

Being eighteen also means you get to go off to college and try living on your own for a while. Be brave, be careful, and be certain that we do want you home for Thanksgiving.

Love,
Mom

It Could Happen to You

On your twenty-first birthday

Dear daughter,

Have I ever told you the story of how I spent my twenty-first birthday? I had been working so hard at the school newspaper, that by the time I flew home to celebrate with the family, all I could do was fall asleep on the living room carpet. Your grandparents were delighted.

Ask Aunt Susan how she spent her twenty-first birthday, and I'm sure you'll agree: I had a more fun, sanitary evening, and no one's suede boots got wrecked.

But seriously. You're entering that part of life where the road you've traveled so far—a relatively straight path—has the potential to bend and fork in all sorts of directions. Many of the curves ahead will come from choices you make—in work, in friendships, and in love. Choose carefully, but with passion. Bad choices generally do not lead to happy destinations, though they certainly will make you a wiser person.

And of course, some curves will just appear in the road without warning. And it's how you deal with them that will determine whether you triumph or wither, crash or continue on. You can't always control what happens to you. But your attitude and heart are yours alone.

Someday, you will know how badly I want every turn your life takes to open the road wide onto a lush and beautiful valley. And how much I want you to run in the fields and find a place that feels like home.

But for now, I'll be happy if you just buckle your seat belt.

Love,

Mom

On your thirtieth birthday

Dear daughter,

Holy crap! I'm sixty years old, so I can use that kind of language without having to apologize. And I'm also realizing something: You owe me a thirtieth birthday party. I spent mine in a La-Z-Boy eating ice cubes and frozen grapes, and wondering just how much stretch I have left in my skin.

Because I am your mother, I want to make this easy on you. Whatever you're doing, I'll just tag along. You won't even notice I'm there. I'll even ride in the back seat.

On second thought (and this has nothing to do with the way you drive—really), I will just stay home with your father. The more I think about it, the more I realize that thirty will be the best birthday I could ever have.

I was about to receive the greatest gift a human could want. Someone to love unconditionally, and without limits. Someone who represented the optimistic belief that the world is a wonderful place for fragile vessels carrying strong souls.

Thinking of the joy and beauty you've brought and all

the anguish I've felt watching you paddle bravely into the rough waters of adulthood makes me weep.

And you know I hate going out when my eyes get all puffy. Have fun tonight.

I love you,
Mom

A Mother's Work Is Never Done

As my pregnant body nears the bursting point, there are two questions people ask me most: "How are you feeling?" and "Are you going back to work?"

The first one's easy. I feel great. It's so bizarre. After months and months of barfing, exhaustion, and general malaise, I finally feel like a normal person again. I know this isn't supposed to happen when you're days from delivery and you look anything but normal. And I also know normal people don't need to use the buddy system to get off the couch.

Whatever the reason, I'm just going to consider myself lucky that I can use a can opener on tuna without contemplating a kitchen C-section.

The second question is a lot harder. I love my job, and the people I work with are like a second family to me, only I don't have to take any of them to the airport at six in the morning.

The truth of the matter is that the people who are asking

this question are probably asking it just to ask. It's a variation on "How are you feeling?" "When is that baby coming?" and "Have you picked a name yet?"

They don't care nearly as much as I do about the answer. So I should probably stop giving myself heartburn every time I try to explain that I still haven't figured out how I will combine parenthood with work. Except that I want to do both.

I know, it's not as if I'm the first person ever to face this question. But that doesn't mean I'm going to take other people's solutions as my own.

Particularly because a lot of solutions are, as we say in the software business, binary. This means there's a yes or no answer. I've had people say, "You don't want to do what your mom did and just bake cookies all day, do you?" Others, meanwhile, have said, "You will find the company of small children to be incredibly boring."

First of all, my mother did a lot more than bake cookies for us. It's an insult to her early life's work to have someone sum it up that way. But that's what a lot of people think stay-at-home moms do. And, if you ask me, those people should go to their rooms and think that over until dinnertime.

Also, I don't find children to be in any way boring. I actually get quite a lot of entertainment just talking to my cat, and cats have a lot less intellectual and emotional range than human beings. That said, I am a little worried about feeling isolated, especially when the baby is crying and I don't know why—or when I start actually caring who the father of Hope's baby is on *Days of Our Lives*.

The thing is, I really, really like work. Since I was sixteen years old, I've never been without a job. And every job I've had has gotten progressively more interesting, which isn't hard when you start out as a strap cutter in a golf-bag manufacturing company. But even that job was fun. I had a task to do, and I liked developing systems for doing it fast and well. I also liked the people I worked with. I would go home stinking of burned rubber, but feeling satisfied with accomplishment—and flush with the $4.00 per hour I was paid.

And let's face it: We can all say kids are more important than money. And they are. But it sure is easier raising them when you have some.

Motherhood is a different kind of work than the kind with paychecks and 401Ks. Yes, you can count loads of laundry that are washed. You can count diapers changed. You can eventually put a "My Kid Beat Up Your Honor Student" bumper sticker on your minivan.

But no one ever says, "Good job on that presentation about why homework is important. You deserve a raise." You just get barfed on in bed. And if you're lucky, a little handmade card with spidery writing that your angel made in nursery school.

The real work of parenthood is something that takes a lifetime to measure, if it can be measured at all. It's an act of faith, really. You give your life to launch someone else's, and trust that the sacrifice of your self-centered ways will pay off in a happy, productive adult who moves out by the time she is, oh say, thirty.

So the question is, can quality parenthood be combined with an invigorating job? It's not a question I'm going to seek an answer to today. I am taking five months off work, which should give me plenty of time to decide. Meanwhile, I got some great advice from a manager on this.

She said, "Don't even think about it until the baby is born. You won't know until you're experiencing it."

That's so true, for so many things.

Momsomnia

There's something really luxurious about being wide awake—*and I mean wide awake*—at 1:43 A.M. two days before your due date.

And that's the sure and comforting knowledge that this is perhaps the last time you will have the luxury of being unable to sleep through the wee hours without having a screaming baby in your arms. At least for a few months, and possibly for a few years, if you decide that parenthood is so great that you want to do it again.

You get to look over at your dear husband sleeping peacefully, snoring gently, and grinding his teeth ever so adorably. You wonder why your cat, which you saved from life on the streets when she was scabby and gross, likes to sleep on his side of the bed. What's wrong with you, anyway, that animals like him more? Well, the cats, anyway. The dog likes you more, but like your husband, she too is snoring gently from her spot on the carpet.

Which you have started noticing lately is covered in spots. Covered in them. Even though it is nigh impossible for you to bend over, and spending extended amounts of time on your hands and knees is not sustainable with life in a world where you still need oxygen, you can't stop working on those spots. This is a time in your life to develop a deep hatred for carpet, and a deeper yearning for hardwood floors, which might actually stand up to a good hosing.

Only you can't afford hardwood floors, not with a baby on the way. Especially since you just had to have the bathtub replaced, because it was leaking into the downstairs neighbor's apartment. But you couldn't replace the bathtub without replacing the tile. And you couldn't replace the tile without repainting. And what do you know, the toilet was installed without a critical part, and you have to replace that part, too (oddly enough, at a cost greater than the actual toilet). And because you're nine months pregnant, you decide it's best to hire someone to do all this work, even though you think of yourself as a thrifty do-it-yourselfer.

This means that you spend time during the day waiting for contractors to show up, while you try to finish up loose ends at work, enjoying the peace and quiet that comes with the jackhammers working on the sidewalk next door.

But those carpet stains are really distracting. So you get on your hands and knees, working on them. Meanwhile, your husband's cat, which is insane, keeps ripping out tufts of his black hair and rubbing them into the filthy carpet, because it's you who are home, and not your husband.

"If only you knew how to use the phone," you say to the cat, "you would do what I do." And that is, call your husband at work. Because you miss him. And because you want to make sure he thinks the shower-curtain rod you picked out will be okay.

And while you're calling him, you realize that in the week you've been away from work, "resting" for the baby's arrival, you've turned into the kind of wife who calls to make sure she got the right shower-curtain rod.

And that is what is so great about insomnia when your baby is on the inside instead of on the outside, demanding food and a clean rump. It gives you time to really get a clear perspective on life, and how yours is about to change.

This is the sort of navel-gazing that I may not have the opportunity to engage in once the baby arrives. And that's only partly because my navel has been stretched so tight it seems to have a stretch mark on it. God help me.

Late pregnancy is not a beautiful thing, at least in the fashion magazine sense of the word. And this is only compounded by your decision to reread all of the "labor and delivery" chapters of your childbirth books.

There are two things you notice. The first is that not all the symptoms you're experiencing match up exactly with the descriptions of things you're reading. One book I read, for example, described the "electric, tingling sensation" women allegedly feel as the baby works her sweet little head lower in your pelvis.

To me, this feels electric only in the sense that an electric bread knife feels electric to a loaf of sourdough. It's more of a slashing feeling, a sensation that prevents me from walking when it strikes. And something I consider a likely indication that the baby has at least one horn, even though my doctor assures me she does not.

The second thing you notice is that there are *truly disgusting* words used for various aspects of childbirth. One of my least favorite terms is "vernix," which is the cheesy, white substance that coats infants as they develop in the womb. I much prefer the term "baby cold cream," which is how one of the more vintage books I read describes it.

Starting now, I am officially on a campaign to end the use of the word vernix. Who's with me? And who else finds the phrase "mucus plug" and its alternative "bloody show" to be among the most frightening ones ever coined? My sister Susan finds it hilarious to call me during the day and ask if I've lost my mucus plug yet.

The only thing worse than this is that I might actually have to call the doctor and report the loss of said mucus plug. Why can't I just say I've popped the cork? Or progressed to Stage Two, or something else that doesn't sound so utterly nasty?

Every night for the past couple of weeks, as I've bobbed off to sleep, like a fat cork in a rough lake, I think to myself, this could be the night. I could wake up in a few hours, electric and tingly with labor.

And like the feeling you get when you're in a plane that's taking off, you know there's nothing you can do but fasten your seat belt and pray for a safe ride. And meanwhile, as the plane soars upward, you look down and see your everyday world shrink into a patchwork quilt. Houses and streets become dots and squares, abstract patterns that are so beautiful they make your eyes sting.

Yes, these are the landmarks of your former life. But they're dwarfed by the trip you've embarked upon. And you can't help but wonder just when and where you will touch down.

Chapter 5

The Birthday

Giving birth is like taking your lower lip and forcing it over your head.

—Carol Burnett

And then afterward, people expect you to smile pretty for the camera.

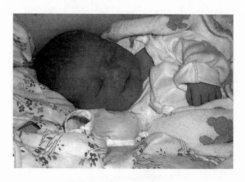

Lucy Jane Berliant

Born August 5, 2000

2:48 P.M.

Seven pounds, 13 ounces, and utterly beautiful

The Birthday

I Remember the Day You Were Born

Now that I'm a parent, there's a family tradition that I can foist upon the next generation. And it's not yard work instead of spring break. At five days old, Lucy is still a bit young for that. And we don't have a yard, anyway.

Rather, the tradition goes like this: When each of our birthdays rolls around, Mom says, "I remember the day you were born."

And then she tells us exactly how it went. Except, now that I've been barefoot down the hot-coal-lined childbirth trail, I swear she's lying. For example, she says having a baby is easier than running a marathon. This is not true. While the last six miles of a marathon do make your legs feel like they are birthing aliens, these aliens are small—maybe two pounds each. And you know exactly when they will be born, down to the mile. You can even project a time, based on your overall pace, which is measured by friendly volunteers with stopwatches and orange wedges.

Childbirth is not like this.

Nor was it like the story my mom used to tell me about the day I was born. I came late, and the labor took less than an hour. Or so she says.

After I passed my own due date, and several days after that, and after I got so huge I could barely get off the couch, and all the while enjoying Seattle's longest heat wave since, well, forever, my doctor asked me a question:

"How would you like to have the baby this week?"

I said, "Yeah."

What I was thinking was, *"Criminy, I wanted this baby to come last week when she was due."*

What she meant, and what I didn't realize, is that I could have the labor induced. I had been expecting to have a middle-of-the-night, blast-the-baby-out-of-the-cannon labor just like Mom. Or maybe even faster—like my marathon time is faster than hers. So, the idea of inducing felt foreign. It was also cheating. But after talking it over with my husband and my folks, I decided to go for it. My dad made the winning argument. Would I rather have an emergency medical procedure, or would I rather have a planned one? Because far too much of my life is an emergency, I opted for planning. This seemed like as good a time as any to get life organized. In hindsight, I think I goofed. Had I just been patient, Lucy, your birthday might have only lasted one day.

But as I will show you many times as you grow up, I am not perfect. And this is what happened on the day you were born. Well, actually, the day before:

Adam and I arrived at the hospital at 7 A.M. on Friday, just like we were supposed to. The people behind the registration desk looked at us blankly when we said we were there for our appointment.

"That's scheduled for Monday," one of them said.

"Sorry," the other said, shrugging.

To put it mildly, politely, and far more serenely than I felt, this was disappointing. But we turned around and went back outside. By the time we had gotten back to the car, we were feeling less obedient. We decided to turn around and see if we could change their minds with a little sweet talk, or maybe with a little help from Mr. Fist. Actually, that's not true. We don't even know a Mr. Fist. But it's fun to think about what would have happened if I'd punched one of those smug registration people. I'm sure I could have done some damage, if I put all my weight into it, because on the day you were born, Lucy, I was about the size and shape of a Volkswagen bug standing on its back tires.

On our return trip, Mr. Fist proved to be entirely unnecessary, because we ran into Dr. Cho, who had scheduled the Friday appointment herself. She set the record straight, and we were back on for 11 A.M. Adam and I went home, tried to nap, and cleaned spots out of the carpet.

After these fruitless endeavors, we returned to the hospital. I needed to remind myself that we wouldn't be leaving without you. Despite being hugely pregnant, and despite all the months leading up to this, it still felt a little unreal, like a Disneyland storefront facade. Also, I didn't see how it was possible that we were going to get you out of me without a chainsaw. Although I tried not to show it, I was scared. I'd done difficult physical things before, but never something with as much at stake. I told myself that only one thing mattered, Lucy: that you were born safe and sound. Well, two things: I also didn't want to swear on videotape.

My first labor nurse, Lois, came in four hours early for her shift to take care of me. How could I not want to perform impressively for someone like that? Lois and Dr. Cho hooked me up to a set of monitors, one for your heartbeat and the other to measure my contractions. Then they applied the gel that was supposed to get labor started, and I spent the next hour or so in bed, waiting for it to take.

After that, I was free to go until later that afternoon. It was a curiously humdrum experience. Here I was, hours from giving birth, but instead of doing something sensible, like writing a will, or momentous, like lighting a candle in church, we had lunch: noodles and butterscotch cookies. If I had to do it over again, I would skip the noodles and the cookies. I'll explain more about this later, when you're having a child of your own.

Then we went to the mall with your aunt Ann and cousin Katy, and bought Katy some back-to-school hiking boots. She was torn between those and a pair of really giant sandals. This made me wonder what kind of shoes you'd want to wear to school. You can have anything you want, Lucy, as long as they're practical. And here's a hint: giant sandals aren't.

All the while we were picking shoes, we timed contractions with your grandma's marathon stopwatch. The contractions were coming every three to six minutes. That got my hopes up. After a few hours of this, it was time for us to head back to the hospital for an exam and more monitoring.

And so began a very long night. Though I was having regular contractions, they weren't opening the baby gate, no matter what I did. I walked up and down the hospital halls for hours. I concentrated on my focal point: a smiley-face sticker Katy stuck to the wall. I took a Jacuzzi tub and missed Katy's departure. But I did get her note: "Please call befor you get clos. Love, Katy. P.S. I am vary exited."

Despite all that, I was closed tighter than a dead clam. Dr. Cho broke the not-surprising news that you wouldn't be coming tonight. Lois took my face in her hands and said, "You're going to get to seven centimeters by morning."

Then Dr. Cho brushed my hair, and Adam and I settled down for some sleep. My second labor nurse, Carolyn, was excellent company during the wee hours, as was Dr. Cho, who made several visits herself. I'm not sure how much I slept and how much I was awake that night. I do know that I was sleeping at one-forty, and awake at one-forty-one, when Adam's cell phone rang. Though we didn't wake up in time to answer it, it was hilarious the next morning hearing your grandmother Carol leave her usual "message marked urgent" voicemail. When Adam dialed in to get the message, I could hear Carol's voice from across the room. She was sure that something was *terribly wrong* because we hadn't phoned. The only thing that was wrong was that the voicemail on her phone didn't work, and she didn't get our message. But you can't blame your grandma for worrying. It's because she loves you, maybe even more than she loves worrying.

At six the next morning, my new labor nurse Lisa hooked me up to a pitocin drip—that's the stuff that really jumpstarts contractions. And it worked. I started getting monster ones.

Except they still weren't opening me up any. They were just making me barf. If only babies could come out the mouth, I would be set. Five hours later—and twenty-four hours after we'd started—I had dilated only two more centimeters.

This was so frustrating. I had trained for this and was doing everything I was supposed to. Taken classes. Visualized. Employed the rocking chair. Walked the halls. Breathed funny. Stared at my happy-face sticker. I had plenty of supportive crewmembers cheering me on.

But this labor was turning out to be actual work. It wasn't that it was horribly painful, although I momentarily thought I was paralyzed after one whopping contraction in my back. Rather, what was making me feel homicidal was the intermittent nausea and the occasional anecdote from my mother about how quick and easy her own labors were. I decided not to kill her, because she's going to be an excellent grandmother to you. Also, I was hooked up to an IV, which limited my mobility. But if I ever have another child, I'm going to make sure Mom's mouth is busy chewing taffy, because she is no longer allowed to tell me how efficiently she popped us out. She gave birth to five children in the time I took to dilate five centimeters.

At that point, I made a decision: This sure would be easier if I a) were put out of my misery or b) had a little pain relief.

Within minutes, an anesthesiologist had me hooked up to a nice epidural block. Boy, that sure made things better. I had hoped for a natural childbirth. It would have been great to be able to say I gave birth then cooked a four-course meal for sixteen. But my own personal ambitions felt really unimportant when I realized I wasn't enjoying your birthday. And now, I can say a hearty amen for anesthesia. I love that stuff!

Your dad says watching me under the influence of it was like looking at a glass being filled with Kool-Aid—apparently, I had been a pretty sick shade of yellow, and the pain relief made my color come back. It also made my feet swell up like popovers, so for the next hour or so, Ann and Susan massaged them. I don't know when I've ever loved my sisters more. It more than makes up for all the clothes they "borrowed" over the years.

Pretty soon, I took a thirty-minute nap. And when I woke up, I had opened up two more centimeters. That left three to go.

My family kept me company for a little while, and then took a lunch break. I used that as an excuse to take another nap— this time, for forty minutes. The kind, thoughtful people in our family (they know who they are) returned from lunch and quietly watched the contractions on the monitor. Apparently, when I was sleeping, they were huge.

While they quietly watched the contraction-monitoring pen scribble mountains, your uncle Andy barged into the room and woke me up. Darrrr! I had been enjoying the nap. But it was a good thing he made that racket, because I was ten minutes away from being dilated enough to push. And while I didn't mind sleeping through labor, I never could have forgiven myself if I slept through your birth.

Dr. Cho cleared everyone but Adam and Nurse Lisa out of

the room. I looked over at the clock. It was 2 P.M. Ten minutes have never passed faster. "*Will this hurt?*" I thought. "*How long will I have to push? Will she be a healthy baby? Will she even be a girl? Those ultrasounds can be wrong, and I have a dresser full of little pink outfits.*"

I felt the fear rise inside me. I momentarily confused it with nausea and made Adam bring the basin. Then I realized I needed to stop thinking this way. Especially about the clothes. Boys can wear pink, after all.

So, I looked at your dad, held his hand, emptied my mind, and got ready to push.

For the next half hour, Dr. Cho, Lisa, and Adam coached and cheered. While Adam counted out seconds, Lisa and Dr. Cho described the progress I was making. I could feel you coming closer and closer to this world, and I could see the top of your head in the little square mirror that Lisa held—at least when it was pointed in the right direction. When it wasn't, I saw part of me I'd never seen before, and hope to never see again. But at least that provided me with the motivation to finish the job.

Pushing was really hard work—but it also was the first phase of labor I felt like I could control. So I went at it like a piranha on the cow that has fallen into the river. I didn't even stop when the phone rang and rang and rang mid-push. (Later, when we listened to the message, we learned it was your aunt Kim, wondering what was up. Let's call her when she's on the cusp of giving birth to her first child, okay, Lucy? She'll love it, I'm sure.)

It felt like no time at all, but thirty-eight minutes later, your head finally emerged. Lisa and Dr. Cho told me to stop pushing for a minute while they cleared your nose and mouth. And then, I got the go-ahead to finish the job.

I was amazed to see your body slip out. You were so much bigger than I expected—nearly eight pounds. Adam's first words were "Whoa. That's a lot of baby." Then, "She's a girl, all right."

And there you were, on my belly, wailing at the world. You didn't cry for long, though. After you were measured and returned to me, your mouth was making an adorable little O shape, and you were sticking out your tongue—as if you were tasting the air.

Lucy, you hadn't been here for five minutes, and already you were asking for something to eat. I held you close to me and in seconds, you had your wish. I had some performance anxiety, of course. The family had returned to the room, and there's nothing quite like breast feeding for the first time ever—in front of your dad. But when you get down to it, there's nothing like feeding your baby for the first time, period.

I looked down at you with your hair still damp, your skin still smelling like hazelnuts, and felt nothing but wonder at your presence. I had waited for you for so long, and here you were, perfect and new. A tiny stranger, but so familiar in the deepest of ways. And of course, so easy to love.

I remember the day you were born, Lucy. A mother was also born that day. She knew life would never be the same again. And she was glad.

Chapter 6

The Fourth Trimester

Nobody has ever measured, not even poets, how much the heart can hold.

—Zelda Fitzgerald

Why is my stomach so big, even though it's no longer holding a baby?

The Houseguest from Hell

It's a good thing no one told me that the day after I'd given birth, I'd be getting a visit from an inconsiderate little houseguest, one who demands food constantly, stays up all hours of the night, and makes rude noises and smells. She doesn't even know how to say thank you for the hospitality I am providing, despite the fact that I am tired, sore, weary, and quite possibly, exhausted. In fact, she doesn't seem to be able to say anything other than, "Unh, unh. Chuff-chuff. Weaaah."

Had anyone warned me, I might have rethought this baby

thing when there was still time. I hear France is nice this time of year. That's where people who don't have newborns go. They drink their wine; they ooze their attitude and flaunt their regular pants. *Mon Dieu*, how I hate those people.

The truth is, the first week of parenthood is a character-building experience. Once you've made it through the trials of labor—which leaves you feeling like you sat on the south side of a lawn mower—you have to bring the baby home. And then you learn that babies are like the world's worst houseguests. They're the relatives you've never met before who take over your house. They make constant demands and have poor communication skills. What's more, they never leave. Apparently, it gets even worse when they become teenagers.

It's a wonder the human race has survived at all. The reason why has to be the same reason we also have dogs and cats among us. Puppies, kittens, and babies are adorable. Lucy is even cute when she cries, which she's doing right now. So far, it has taken me more than a week to write about the first week of parenthood. Excuse me while I feed her.

Okay. I'm back.

That took longer than it reads.

If you were to map out the first week of parenthood, it would have exactly two distinguishing features: the mountain known as "Getting to Know Baby" and the river known as "Sleep, Ahhh, Sleep." Only the river has dried up. So, it's really all about climbing that mountain, without benefit of

Sherpas or oxygen. Worse, your shirt is off most of the time, and documentary photographers follow you everywhere.

Because babies can't talk, your efforts at understanding who they are and what they want are pretty limited at first. The first step in understanding the mystery creature in your arms is to figure out who she looks like: you or her daddy. This is a mistake, of course. Just because she looks like your husband doesn't mean she's going to bring you breakfast in bed. Still, you think perhaps her looks are a window into her character, so you study them closely, anyway.

You will have help in this task. Most people who stop by to eat your postpartum cookies will tell you, "Your baby's beautiful! And she looks *just* like your husband." Which you think is probably true, but you interpret it as a sly commentary on how crummy you look these days. That excuse you'd been using— "I'm nine and a half months pregnant"—no longer does you any good. It's depressing. A neighbor just asked me, "Did you get a new stroller?" I said, "Yes. Would you like to see the baby inside it?" And she replied, "Oh. I didn't realize you'd had it."

Why is it that no one ever told me I'd look pregnant *after* the baby came?

But back to the baby's looks. Apparently, it's an evolutionary advantage for babies to look like their fathers. It proves the baby is theirs. You don't need proof to know who the mother is. Just find the crying woman who still looks pregnant and really needs to sit down but can't because of a lawnmower incident.

Based on the ultrasound, I was kind of expecting Lucy to look like me. I don't know why. I've never seen my face bones, and lately, they've been surrounded by what looks like a flesh mattress. Still, Lucy's skull was awfully cute and girly. I took this to mean that she'd look like me. So, it was a bit of a surprise to gaze at this little face and say, "Good Lord. Was I even swimming in the gene pool when Lucy was conceived? She looks exactly like Adam."

I even got a picture of myself as a newborn to compare. And, sure enough, there is no resemblance. By comparison, I look like the Missing Link: Even as a baby, I had very well-defined eyebrows and a giant mouth. Lucy and Adam both have little mouths that open in exactly the same way when they're sleeping. She also has his coffee-bean brown eyes. And her diaper is always falling down—a problem Adam has with his pants due to his rear end, which is the size and shape of a squashed hamburger bun.

The biggest difference that I can see is that Lucy is much more of a boob man than Adam ever was. You can tell by the way she eats. Before she latches on, she makes a sound like an engine revving, and she shakes her head back and forth. Then she hangs on like a lamprey and doesn't let go for anything. You can hear her eat from across the room. From the looks on their faces, I suspect my visitors feel sorry for me.

For Lucy, though, the technique seems to be paying off. Doctors are usually happy when babies regain any lost birth weight by their two-week mark. Lucy had gained almost a pound by the time she was one week old. This is because, in my attempts to understand her, I have figured out what one sound means: the hungry cry. It is a sound I hear a lot—at least every two hours, interspersed with what I think is the wet cry and the burp-me wail. At two in the morning, of course, all of these cries sound pretty much the same. So I try a little of everything until something works. More often than not, a little drink is all she needs to feel better.

It's a good thing Lucy is so lovable, or I would probably lose hope and faith, though not my appetite. You can love your newborn with all your heart, but she can't yet give you the one thing you live for: a smile, a genuine, this-isn't-just-gas smile. You can be sure I'm counting the days until that happens.

Welcoming Wishes

Before Adam and I got married, we made a deal: Any children we had, not including the pets, would be raised in the Jewish faith.

When we made this pact, it seemed like the best way to have Lucy understand her father's religious heritage. This is because Adam and I live in the same town as my Catholic family; we say a Catholic blessing before Sunday dinners; we celebrate Christmas and Easter with my folks. His family, meanwhile, lives halfway across the country, blowing the shofar and eating unleavened bread at the appropriate and meaningful times.

Of course, deals like this are easy to make, and a lot harder to implement. If your baby is a girl, there isn't a time-honored way to welcome her into the world. I don't regret the fact that she won't be circumcised, of course. But it did mean I was going to have to make up a ceremony.

And that was just fine by me. I love taking parts of various religions and creating something meaningful out of them, like a religious crazy quilt. For example, a Catholic priest and a Jewish sex expert performed Adam's and my wedding. It was a great ceremony, and nowhere near as naughty as it sounds.

For the baby, though, I wanted something really special. Catholics baptize new babies in holy water, and Jews hold naming ceremonies for girls. These things became the foundation for our ceremony, which would be delightfully free of blood.

I knew one person singularly well qualified to lead my family in welcoming Lucy to the world: my high school art teacher, who had offered to do a newborn welcoming ceremony when he found out Lucy was on the way. This was the art teacher who let us write on the walls, the man who took a group of students on a weeklong trip in a Winnebago, and the guy who gave me a really fun summer job after my senior year, when I was desperate for employment and money for college. That summer job was one of the best I ever had—it was right before this teacher's first book came out: *All I Really Need to Know, I Learned in Kindergarten.*

Now, people think of him as the world-famous author Robert Fulghum. But to me, he'll always be the guy who encouraged me to be creative and to think deeply, especially about the things that matter most—other people. He's also the one, through his actions, who inspires me to be generous and useful to others. His example is impossible to live up to, but it keeps me trying. I started by reading Fulghum's book on rituals. It's called *From Beginning to End: The Rituals of Our Lives,* and should be required reading for anyone who wants to live an examined, thoughtful life. There's a great section describing how a baby named Max is welcomed into a neighborhood—and how the ceremony turned the guests into neighbors, as opposed to people who just lived near each other.

I wanted Lucy's welcoming ceremony to focus on family, and to take a little inspiration from one of my favorite fairy tales, *Sleeping Beauty.* I always liked the part where the fairy godmothers gave the newborn girl wishes, even if one wish by an uninvited guest turned out pretty ugly. All babies should be blessed by magic. When Adam and I issued invitations, we asked all the participants to bring Lucy their wish for her life.

Then Fulghum and I sat down and talked about what other things we wanted to include. We decided that I would explain how Lucy got her name, that we'd talk about our family origins, and that we'd burn a special candle made especially for Lucy by a friend. And finally, we would pour water on a tree that we'll plant for Lucy, and then "baptize" her in something—just not the traditional oil or water.

So, when Lucy was just thirteen days old, we gathered together at my parents' house to welcome her to the world.

Fulghum first invited my grandma to talk about what my mother was like as a baby. We learned that my grandfather had been off fighting World War II at the time. And then my mom talked about what I was like. This story I knew: I was a lovely, sweet baby. And she has no idea what happened to make me turn out like I did.

Then I explained how we chose the name Lucy Jane. We had three reasons: Lucy means light, while Jane means God is gracious. I love the optimism of the combination. What's more, neither name is very common today, and we wanted Lucy to always feel like an individual. Jane also happens to be the name of Adam's beloved aunt. And finally, my godmother, who died two years ago from Alzheimer's, was named Lucille. She became my godmother not long after her husband and son died. And I wanted to acknowledge the memory of this amazingly courageous woman—as well as the cycle of life and death.

Holding Lucy and explaining the origins of her name made me cry. I think it's because the name is one of those things that make a baby feel real. Choosing a name is one of the most concrete things a parent can do for a child. It's the first symbol of the individual life that has been created, and I think why baby-naming ceremonies came to be.

Naming Lucy felt a little like the Hmong soul-calling ritual performed for newborns: It's a first invitation for the baby's essence as a human being to enter. And here we were, inviting a beam of light into the fold, a beam that had traveled across generations on the gentle wings of a gracious God.

But that wasn't the only time I cried at Lucy's welcoming ceremony. My eyes stung with each wish that my family and friends bestowed. Not only were the wishes beautiful but the individuality of them reminded me how very lucky I am to have such people around me. If all of the wishes for Lucy come true, she will live a charmed life indeed.

She'll feel beautiful, find and follow a passion, have deep friendships with family and friends. She'll have a teacher who changes her life. She'll feel peace, patience, love, and understanding; she'll listen to the rhythm and music of life; she'll have courage, and she'll laugh often. She will like getting her hands dirty in gardens, both literal and metaphoric. And like the Velveteen Rabbit, she will let life's rough patches make her real, instead of breaking her spirit.

If my wish for her comes true, she will live her life being true to herself, and knowing that each day is a gift. I've never felt that so much in my life as I do now, savoring the first few days of my daughter's life, where all is potential, all is hopeful, and my only responsibility is to love.

Of course, bestowing this wish on Lucy made me cry all over again. Just in time for her to mess her diaper loud enough for everyone to hear.

With that, Fulghum administered the final ritual—anointing Lucy's head. "We've chosen a special substance," he said. "Something that runs in all our veins."

And he took out a small dish of peanut butter, and dotted it on her forehead. Welcome to the world, Lucy. May your life always be so rich, nourishing, and in the best way, thoroughly nutty.

Parenthoia

Motherhood, I am learning, is all about doing things you had vowed not to do. Though I haven't bought a minivan yet, nor do I wipe things off Lucy's face with a spit-covered finger, I'm sure it's just a matter of time.

One promise I'd made to myself is that I would not be so paranoid that I'd need to check Lucy's breathing every time her eyes were closed. "Babies are tough!" I used to say.

I no longer say such things. Not only do I feel for her breathing, I put my head by her nose and listen for it. I watch her little chest rise and fall. I squeeze her hands to see if I can get some sort of life-affirming reaction—all while trying to make sure she stays asleep.

I don't know what it is about the sight of your own newborn that sends sanity right out the window. But I know it is a fact of life, just as certain as the awkwardness of adolescence. And it can make a mom do strange things.

It Could Happen to You

For example, a few days after Lucy was born, my brothers and sisters came over to admire her. My younger brother, a doctor, immediately started testing all of her reflexes and touching the soft spot on her head. Now, had he been just a regular doctor—as opposed to the kid who stepped on our other brother's birthday cake one year—this probably wouldn't have freaked me out. In fact, doctors regularly check infants' reflexes to make sure they have good muscle tone.

But watching Andy do this was like having someone put a worm down my shirt. And so, in front of everyone, I told him to knock it off in the rudest possible way. Right away, I felt horrible. Andy went out on the porch and started looking at a bonsai tree he'd given my husband, and I went out to apologize—and, self-righteously, to ask him never to test her reflexes again. It wasn't much of an apology, I'm afraid. And what Andy said has stuck with me: "You have to accept me as I am."

He's right, of course. He's a doctor. He's interested in how the body works. And he knows what he's doing. And I know he loves her as much as I love him.

But once you are a parent, accepting other people—and the world—as they are is not always so easy. All you want is for your child to be loved by everyone and safe at all times. Two impossible goals. Too much to ask, but you do it anyway.

Especially when everything seems to be going wrong.

After a quiet, happy morning when Lucy was ten days old, she turned into a different baby by afternoon. She spit up huge quantities of goo, so much that I wasn't sure it could still be called spit-up. Instead of her usual rusty-door-hinge cry, she wailed and shrieked like she was in some sort of pain. For hours, she cried and cried. All afternoon, I tried everything to console her, but nothing was working. Not walking, rocking, singing, cuddling—and certainly not the crib. I was afraid to feed her, for fear she'd barf again. But even when I tried, she would only eat for a few seconds, and then start up again with the wailing.

My sister Susan made it home from work around 5 P.M. and came over to help. She managed to get Lucy to stop crying for a while. But by 7, when Adam was home, Lucy was still screeching. So I called the pediatrician and told the nurse on call what was going on.

Because Lucy had barfed twice, she recommended we go to the emergency room. Adam, Susan, and I packed up the little wailing baby and set off for the hospital.

When we arrived, the waiting room was full of children in varying states of distress. Some looked perfectly healthy. I learned later those were the three boys under three years old who had swallowed rocks.

Others did not look so fortunate. There was one girl, who looked like she was around thirteen years old. She sat in a wheelchair, as thin and pale as a ghost. And there was an infant, I couldn't tell how old, who just didn't look right. By comparison, Lucy was in great shape. But I was still desperate to know why she was screaming.

So for four hours, we stayed at the hospital, while three different doctors looked in her ears, her eyes, and other openings. They took the blood pressure in all four extremities. They listened to her heart and her lungs, and they felt her arteries. And finally, they brought her back into the bowels of the hospital for a chest X ray.

Seeing my tiny, naked baby on her back, her arms and legs weighed down by sandbags, her pelvis covered by a lead apron, and screaming herself purple, was awful. She looked as though she was being crucified. And I had to stand behind a glass window to watch, while hot tears uncontrollably oozed down my cheeks.

Luckily, everything turned out to be just fine. In my inexperience, I made much ado about nothing. Unlike the seriously ill children I saw that day, Lucy woke up the next morning feeling just fine. Unlike other mothers who lose their children, whether in childbirth or later down the line, I still have a perfect little baby to hold.

Life can be so brutally unfair, so mysteriously perverse. Because not all of my years have been happy ones, I've lately felt humbled by my good fortune. And for the same reason, I don't have any illusion that Lucy will be untouched by sadness. Just as I have to accept my goofy brother the way he is, so too do I accept this part of life. I'll love the good parts and the great people, like my brother. And I won't look at either as something I deserve.

That's the only way, I think, to truly appreciate such things as healthy babies. Keeping them safe and healthy is hard work, of course. But not nearly so hard as losing them.

Incidentally, Lucy's day in the hospital was also the first time she cried real tears. How I wish it were the last.

The Baby Boom

People always say that kids grow up so fast. For people who don't have kids, that concept is as easy to grasp as a Swedish movie about the nature of life and death.

That's because when we grew up, it took forever. The last week before Christmas, for example, lasted an average of 57 days during my childhood. The school year, meanwhile, took 1,109 days—1,136 on leap years.

The speed of time changes when you have a baby.

Then, you get a firsthand look at what truly fast growth is. By her four-week checkup, Lucy had grown almost two inches and put on more than three pounds.

At night, when I listen closely, I swear I can hear the pings and pops of her bones and muscles lengthening. Either that, or it's my ruined abdomen trying to return to its former "flattish" shape. But I don't think that's the case, because—as Lucy does nothing but gain weight—I do nothing but fail utterly to lose it. The act of putting my pants on is like stuffing two cougars into a bag. The topic of my porky body is off-limits until I sleep through the night again, though. There's only so much a person can handle at once when terribly sleep-deprived.

I would have thought that I'd shrink as quickly as Lucy is growing. She's like a fungus. I turn my eyes and foomp! She's bigger. No wonder babies cry and sleep so much. It's got to hurt to grow so quickly—and on a liquid diet, no less.

And about that liquid diet: It doesn't exactly stick to her ribs. I had read somewhere that newborns fed every two hours. That sounded fine to me. But that was because I didn't stop to do the math. If a newborn eats for thirty to forty-five minutes out of every two-hour block, that leaves Mom with maybe an hour or so to recover. Meanwhile, baby needs to be burped and changed during that recovery time. And I don't mean just a diaper change. Lucy regularly has what Adam and I call a blowout. That's when Lucy not only requires a new diaper but also a bath, a new outfit, and possibly a change of sheets and other bedding. All this changing can be very upsetting to any baby, which means she will cry and require fifteen minutes of soothing before she's comfortable again. This leaves a grand total of two minutes between nursing sessions. And this is when I shower, eat breakfast, take the dog out, and bake cookies. Wait. I don't bake cookies. That whole myth about stay-at-home mothers baking cookies? Lies, damn lies.

What I've learned in these few weeks is that no matter how many times I read *What to Expect When You're Expecting,* there's no way to know what raising a newborn will be like without actually doing it, and there's no way to understand how quickly it all happens without experiencing it.

Here are more things I didn't expect:

Babies can be picky. I thought they were like those little dolls I used to play with—the kind that didn't care whether they slept on their backs, sides, or in a shoe box. Lucy really likes to sleep on her side, and she cries, wiggles, and kicks at night until I position her just so. Then she falls asleep in about the time it takes a person to snap off a light switch.

Their crying is not annoying. This is so weird. When I was a baby-sitter, it used to set my hair on fire to hear my charges cry. I hated it. Now, my only thought is, *"What's wrong, and how can I fix it?"* And I'm not even getting paid the $1.00 an hour I used to make.

They make crazy eating noises. When Lucy eats, she arches her back, flails her hands, kicks her feet, and makes happy grunts, squeals, and groans. If I close my eyes, I can almost imagine I'm feeding a piglet.

And that's not all. She belches and farts like a man. I would not have thought this acoustically possible. It's quite startling—for both of us.

She doesn't like classical music. I don't know how I'm ever going to raise a Mensa member this way, but Lucy far prefers Disney music.

Pacifiers suck. But not in the good way. Lucy hates the taste. Adam wonders why they aren't more anatomically correct. He has a point there, although I hate thinking about the secondary market for pacifiers like that. Now that I'm a mother, and just starting out my career as a disciplinarian, I can officially say things like that are naughty.

Naked Bliss

Lucy already seems to have some naughty plans for her future. She's let us know, rather clearly, that she plans to be a nudist. Or, as they like to be called, a "naturist," a term I learned from a nudist at work who one told me about a canoe trip she took with her cheeky comrades. The image hasn't given me a moment's peace since. But I'm trying to get used to such things, because Lucy loves to be one with nature.

Sometimes, when she's crying really, really hard, I change her diaper, whether it needs it or not. The moment she feels fresh air on her artistic parts, she stops crying. She also loves her bath time, and only starts crying once I get the towel wrapped around her. If it sounds like there is an awful lot of crying going on in my household, it's true. And I'm not even the one doing most of it. Lucy is a huge crybaby.

She cries when I'm putting her in her Baby Bjorn, which is a cloth baby carrier that hangs down my front and is the closest I've come lately to receiving a Swedish massage. But that's only because poor Adam is as tired as I am, and I haven't been separated from Lucy long enough to even say massage, let alone have one.

Back to crying, though. Lucy cries when she's eating. She cries when she's not eating. She cries when she needs to burp. She cries when she needs to fart. She cries when she's wet. She cries when we're riding in the car. She cries when she's falling asleep. And my favorite, she cries when she's waking up. She can be sound asleep, and in one second, she opens her little mouth and screams something that can only mean, *"Mother of God! I'm awake!"*

Yesterday, Lucy cried so much that she exhausted herself and actually slept four hours into the night, a new record. Which was a good thing, because I was about ready to cry myself.

There are three things that have gotten me through all this crying: Lucy's love of nudity, the dairy farm that's just below my neck, and my family members, all of whom take turns holding her when she's going on a bender.

Well, make that four things. The fourth has been the hope that someday, Lucy will do more than cry. Someday, she will smile.

There is nothing cuter than a smiling baby. This is why you see them all the time on TV, along with women who have nineteen-inch waists and forty-two-inch chests. Like these women, googly, happy newborns are fake. Real babies yowl constantly and pee everywhere. They're like tomcats. But at least they don't shed or cause kittens.

Still, I really did want the kind of baby I'd seen on TV. For the first month we were each other's constant companions, I watched her mouth for signs of a smile. When I would kiss her cheeks, Euro-style, her lips would form a little O, like a baby bird opening for the worm. But that wasn't quite a smile. When I would rattle a toy, her eyes would widen and sometimes she would open her mouth. Again, not quite a smile.

A few times, I've thought she was smiling—only to watch the grin turn into a grimace, accompanied by the symphonic bleat of her diaper being filled. So, it was sweet news indeed, on the day she turned five weeks old, when Adam reported that she had smiled on her changing table. And it was a real smile, he said. She made it when he made a funny sound. And she did not need a new diaper afterward.

My sister and I got a glimpse of a smiling Lucy late that night, as we changed her and put her into her pajamas. Her rosy lips opened wide, her eyes sparkled in the soft light of the nursery, and she flashed her naked gums. I couldn't help myself; I laughed out loud at the sight. It was one of the most delightful moments I've lived, seeing the brand-new look of joy on the tiny face of a child—my child.

It's with moments like this that I'm starting to realize where the best parts of life can be found. They're at the corners, the turning points. It's like when you go outside on a sunny day and take a deep breath and realize it's not summer air you've taken in. There's a snap to it, and you realize that summer has given way to fall, and you're suddenly overwhelmed with happiness at the change, for it symbolizes simple, new pleasures to come: cups of cider, crackling fires, and cozy sweaters.

Lucy's first smile is just like this. It's a forerunner to her first laugh, the first taste of future joy. It's like the horizon swallowing the sun on a glorious cantaloupe-colored evening. It's naked bliss. It overwhelms me.

What's That Smell?

"Do you realize," Adam said as we passed the KFC near our condo, "Lucy has no idea what that smell is?"

That's right. Lucy has no context for the smell of fried chicken, of untold amounts of delicious grease, and of the eleven secret herbs and spices that make Kentucky Fried Chicken one of the most recognizable olfactory experiences on the planet. It's practically nose pornography, and our little Lucy has no idea what to make of it.

Or so we think. There may be something deeply human that recognizes the seductive power of fatty foods. She might recognize it as something great that she'd love to try, if only her gums were up for it.

But she has no way of telling us that, just as there is no way that scent means to her what it means to me: memories of summer boat trips with my family. We'd load up in our crummy orange-and-white powerboat with a bucket of chicken. Just a bucket of chicken, mind you. Drinks were *too expensive*. So we'd eat our drumsticks and gaze at the undrinkable lake water, panting softly. Quite frequently, the boat would break down, and we'd have to paddle to shore. Even so, we couldn't wait for the next trip.

Every day with a newborn is a chance to watch a human being experience something magical for the first time. Last week, for example, Lucy and I were getting ready to take a walk. I had her all strapped in her little cloth carrier when, suddenly, I felt raindrops on my head and hands.

They were just little drops, little warm pats—the first that had fallen since Lucy was born. It was the kind of rain that I ordinarily really like because it means I don't have to water the plants on the balcony.

This time, though, I wasn't so pleased. I still have a tendency to treat Lucy like she's dry-clean only.

"Rain!" I thought. *"Lucy will get wet! And she doesn't have a hat!"*

And there was the distinct possibility that the rain was going to make her cry. But I was in for a happy surprise. Not only was she perfectly fine—no shrinking, no pilling, no fad-ing—she was looking up at the sky with her round, brown eyes and her mouth open wide. When a drop landed on her lip, she tasted it.

Even though babies tend to funnel all new experiences through their mouths, it still gave me a splash of pleasure and pride to see her drink in nature. I could imagine her, all grown up, as an outdoor adventurer, kayaking deftly down the Amazon in search of a plant that would cure a disease that has plagued me all my life: extreme shortness.

Especially when you're home alone with the baby, you tend to imagine all sorts of things with every first you notice, whether it's a first experience—like the smell of chicken or the taste of rain—or a developmental milestone. Baby books list these developmental milestones in great detail. These are the things your baby should be doing in any given week.

When Adam and I first brought Lucy home, we were the stereotypically proud parents. We believed sincerely she was able to do things that babies generally don't do at such a tender age. She was tracking toys with her eyes and holding her head rock steady. And I'm pretty sure she was adding complex sums quietly in her head, because she often had a fiercely contemplative expression that, in my experience, generally only occurs on people doing math. She often required a diaper change after her mental math sessions, which could be quite a source of stress for her in elementary school. But it's nothing that plastic pants can't take care of.

Lucy performed a truly precocious act when she was a mere

five and a half weeks old: She rolled over on her own. And then she repeated the performance five times, while an audience of grandparents, cousins, aunts, and uncles clapped and cheered. We have it preserved forever on videotape. Babies aren't expected to roll over on their own until they're about three months old. So, almost as soon as Lucy demonstrated her exceptional skill in this area (and shamed my dog, who has never been able to do this on command), Adam and I started discussing the future of someone with such exceptional strength. Lucy, we thought, will become a weight lifter, or perhaps a professional bodybuilder. We could just picture her big, round head atop an oiled and muscular body.

"When she gets hair," Adam said, "we will have to give her a perm and cut it into a mullet, so she fits in."

Once the talk got to Lucy's hairstyle, I started realizing we were perhaps taking her rolling ability too far. Maybe it's because I hope she never gets a perm, or maybe it's because I think I would freak out to see her greased up in a bikini, pumping her pecs for an international audience. The thought of being the mother of Arnoldine Schwarzenegger is enough to snap anyone out of this kind of daydream.

Lucy's a baby, but not for long. And I'm planning to enjoy every second of it, something that will be easier if the grease I'm imagining is on my chicken, and not on my child.

How to Dress a Baby

One event of parenthood I looked forward to most was the chance to put those precious, pint-sized baby clothes to good use.

And I do not use this word "event" lightly. Because it is an event, not unlike a combination of gymnastics, weight lifting, and mud wrestling. Only, it's not mud involved, not outdoor mud, anyway.

Lucy muddies several outfits a day. Which means that Adam and I are getting much better at dressing her, even though that's not saying a whole lot.

As with most sports, champion baby dressers start at an early age, using the equipment commonly known as Barbie. This sport's popularity explains why Mattel is a $4.5 billion company. This is larger than the gross domestic product of many small countries, which doesn't seem right for something so anatomically unlikely.

Nonetheless, it explains why I am not a champion baby dresser. I only had one Barbie when I was little: the wholesome, unsexy "Malibu" model. She didn't even come with pumps. Only a lousy pair of sandals. Stupid Malibu.

Because my parents are not the shopping type, and because I never did anything to deserve it, I never got new outfits for Malibu. The one pair of high-heeled Barbie shoes I stole from a friend, I couldn't resist chewing on. They were like everlasting jelly beans. Much like the mythological Sirens seduced seafaring ancient Greeks with their sweet song, those luscious molded plastic pumps shrieked for a good biting. Needless to say, neither sailors nor shoes had much of a chance. Before long, in a totally unrelated fashion, Malibu lost her head, and that was that.

As a result, the adult me is not a skilled dresser. One former boyfriend, whom I did not marry for obvious reasons, called me "Wrinkle Girl." And during my pregnant months, relatives had to perform a fashion intervention because my pants were falling down while my shirts were riding up. I looked like I ate the moon, and these caring people were right to spare innocent bystanders the sight.

Now, Lucy suffers for my deficiency. It's not that I haven't tried to do better. And it's not that I haven't had help. I have zillions of adorable little outfits for her. The problem is, I'm having a really hard time putting them on her.

There is one big reason for this: her head. Newborn heads are not only the size of ostrich eggs; they also suggest a similar fragility. It's as if Humpty Dumpty, with a soft spot on the back of his shell, has come to rest on baby's little shoulders, and all the king's horses and all the king's men are just standing around on a smoking break waiting to say, "I told you so."

Like all newborns, Lucy's head has two soft spots on them. A newborn's soft spot has been a zone of terror for me ever since my youngest sister was born and my mother told me to be careful of it. An errant finger could poke through a soft spot as if it were Jack Horner's pie, I thought. Only a stuck-in thumb wouldn't pull out a plum. It would pop her brain. As a result, I steered clear of Susan's head, and like to think I deserve the credit for all her good grades in school. Of course, I know Lucy's brain won't pop if I touch her soft spot. But I can see her pulse throbbing in it, and I'll be damned if I'm going to cut off the blood supply by pulling a T-shirt on over it.

Also, the first time I tried to dress her, she screamed.

The solution has been to pull all of her clothes on starting at her feet. Yes, this has led to some stretched-out necks on some outfits. But I say the Flashdance look is due for a comeback. It's not a perfect solution, to be sure. This is because Lucy is still able to go fetal on me. I guess, after forty-one weeks of being folded like an origami frog, Lucy retains much of her prebirth flexibility. She can clasp her feet as if in prayer, and she can bring the holy bundle up to her chin. And she does this, regularly, while I tug her onesie from her feet to her neck.

Flies don't know how good they've got it, bearing maggots. I could slip a maggot into a onesie in no time flat. But no. Lucy has an incredibly strong pair of wings that give me all sorts of trouble. For once I am not exaggerating when I say her arms are strong. Jane Fonda nothing. Infantercize with Lucy would make a great workout video. I dare anyone to try lying on his or her back for more than two hours a day, kicking and flailing simultaneously. This workout would leave an

NFL player weeping, I'm sure, after only twenty minutes. But Lucy can't get enough of it.

I've invented a little song called "Where Are Lucy's Hands?" that I sing whenever I get to the final part of baby dressing. I guess I'm pretty literal when I'm under stress, because when I sing this song, I really am looking hard for them. She's flexible and wiggly enough that it can be hard to tell where they've gone.

Though it calms me, the song doesn't really help. That's because Lucy doesn't really know she's Lucy yet, and hands— well, if she knew what those were, she might stop hitting her face with them when she got hungry. I sometimes give up on the song and have Adam finish the job. And that's a really good use of a husband. Let him finish what he started. I mean, really. I had to do the childbirth part.

People tell me that before long, babies really start to like getting dressed. I believe it—Lucy loves getting her diaper changed.

For now, though, Lucy and I both have a favorite outfit— and it's not the little red-and-white-checked dress I bought before I realized that it's the size of a napkin and rides up around her neck. It's her birthday suit. In it, she is perfection. Smooth skin, infinite folds, growing and changing every day. I'd let her wear it more often, if only she'd promise to stop peeing on me.

Dads Don't Mind (Another One by Adam)

There's a secret language that men have. I'm not talking about backward codes that old-timers use at the Moose Lodge to order spiked punch, or the facial expressions men sometimes share when the TV camera (finally!) pans to the cheerleaders.

Yes, those are men's languages. But as I'm sure you know, they're not all that secret. I swear, this one is different. Some strange biological twist has given men the ability to deliver information in a certain way—characterized by a serious tone, a stillness of body language, and a particular look in the eye—that says: *No matter what lies I've ever told, no matter what nonsense I've ever claimed to be fact, no matter how stubborn or stupid I've ever been in the past, what I'm about to say is absolutely, positively the truth.*

Maybe it was evolution's way of giving men the ability to say, "No, there really is a bear in that cave."

I don't know, perhaps women have this language, too. But I do know that as the day our baby was born came closer and closer, I heard that secret language with an unprecedented frequency. From men I knew well, from acquaintances, from strange men in parking lots.

"You better get your sleep now. You're never going to sleep again," this total stranger said to me, in the secret language, just after Martha turned the corner out of earshot at the mall.

"Don't make any plans to do anything after the baby is born. Your whole life is going to change," this other guy said to me, in the secret language, as I was getting coffee at work. "Go out now. Go out to dinner and a movie every night, because you won't be able to later," said one of my best friends, in the secret language, when he realized Martha was in her final weeks of pregnancy.

It scares you when you're a father-to-be, because typically a guy simply dismisses the advice of other men. Not because they don't give good advice, but because that's just the way we are. I don't need you; I don't need to bond—go away. But you keep getting warnings like these in secret language—each time you're thinking, *Oh crap, he's serious*—and you start to wonder, just a little. Is fatherhood going to be like the time I ate bran muffins and Italian prunes right before the road trip across the state?

But now I'm a father, the baby is fantastic of course, and I'm definitely not scared anymore. And per the legitimacy of the secret language, all those things I was told have in fact turned out to be true. Sleep is scarce, free time even scarcer, and the rest of my gray hair will probably come in before I get to the next movie theater.

But the thing is, there's a little phrase that all these friends, strangers, and acquaintances left out: ". . . but you won't mind."

"You're never going to sleep again, but you won't mind," is what that guy should have said. "Your whole life is going to change, but you won't mind."

This "you won't mind" phenomenon, in my opinion, is

the fourth most amazing thing about being a new father. Most amazing is the child herself, second most amazing is the amount of liquid waste the child can generate, third most amazing is how darn cute the little bean is. But fourth, definitely, is how nothing she does can really ever bother you.

When she cries furiously, starting exactly at the time you get dinner ready, you just don't mind. You barely even think of it as crying. When she has a poop blowout over you, your furniture, and her clothes only moments after you just cleaned up the last blowout, you really don't mind. And when she insists that the only comfortable way to take a two-hour nap is on your left shoulder, while bouncing gently just so, it turns out . . . you really don't mind.

I shouldn't be surprised, actually.

A fifth-grade classmate of mine named Liz was something of a pollster. She was the one who would take notes on who liked whom, compile votes on who was the most popular, and ask philosophical questions like, "Could your dad beat up that other kid's dad?"

Liz had what she called a love test. She'd ask which girl in class you loved, and then sharply follow up your answer with a real toughie: "Okay, so, would you pick her nose?"

If you said yes, then you were really in love. If you said no, then you were a faker and didn't deserve her.

Fathers to be, I have yet another message for you, and I'm speaking to you with a serious tone, no body language, and a familiar look in my eye: Get ready. You will have to pick your baby's nose.

And you won't mind.

Becoming a Mother

About two weeks before Lucy was born, I realized I was going to have a baby. I knew I was pregnant, of course. We had those three tests, after all. What's more, I had grown huge. *Huge.* Every part of me was pregnant. My hands were winter-glove puffy. My legs could have supported a large stove. And my neck made me look like an East-European weight lifter after a bowl of Steroid Smacks.

Still, I hadn't fully come to grips with the fact that this pregnancy thing would lead to my having an actual baby. I'd had a vague idea this would be happening, of course. We'd emptied out our "crap room" and turned it into a nursery and filled it with clothes and all sorts of stuff for babies. I'd talked to the dog about it, and I'd even studied Martha Stewart's guide to baby washing.

But there's a big difference between being pregnant and being ready to look this kid in the eye and say, "Because I said so, that's why." And, two weeks before Lucy arrived, I suddenly wasn't so sure I wanted to do this anymore. Not only did I convince myself that, in fact, I could spend the rest of my life looking like I ate a linebacker, I also told Adam repeatedly that he could have the baby. She was all his. Yep. Not mine. Didn't want her. Wake me up when it's over, okay? Thanks.

The bottom line is, I was afraid of losing the life I really enjoyed, and I was afraid I wouldn't know what to do with Lucy once she was here.

Mother Nature gave me a helpful boost by pumping yet more water into my system. This made my ears start to pulse and glow, like warning beacons on a runway. And it was enough to make me say uncle to my overdue pregnancy. But I wasn't quite ready to say mother yet.

Not until Lucy was born. And then, suddenly, I didn't want to put her down. She was beautiful. She was perfect. She had sucking talent—her first sign of what I'm sure will be a lifetime of virtuosity. And I was so glad she was here that I insisted Adam share her, after all.

But this feeling was nothing compared to what I feel these days. I knew I was a mother, but I didn't yet feel like a Mom. And there's a big difference. Mothers give birth, but Moms sustain life. I'm beginning to feel like I can do that. I'm not there yet, of course. But I no longer feel as though Lucy is a mysterious animated doll, perhaps capable of rising up and hog-tying the cats in the night.

It felt like it took forever to get here. One of the baby books I read said that most parents understand their baby's cries after three weeks. That wasn't reassuring at all. Not only was I really tired and pretty much useless when she was three weeks old, I also had only a fuzzy idea of what she needed. Because the book said I should have known better, I was a confirmed failure. As a failure, all I would do to soothe her was try a little of everything. I actually nursed her and changed her diaper simultaneously once. And once is the number of times I will ever do *that*.

Eventually, though, I started noticing some patterns. Once I got those down, I understood Lucy's own private language. This took a good six weeks. I was slow, but I finally got there.

What used to just sound like, "Chuff. Chuff, chuff, chuff," miraculously revealed itself to mean, "I could use something to eat."

"Reeee!" means, "I have a belly full of gas. Help me out here."

"We-ahhh we-ahh *we-aah we-aaah!*" translates to, "Dammit, I'm tired. I could also use something eat. But I'm so very tired that I will fall asleep within minutes of sucking. And then I will get hungry again a few minutes later, wake up, and start shrieking. Get used to it. I'll do it every night around seven P.M., or whenever you and Dad sit down to eat your dinner."

Also, any crying that occurs after she's been fed but before she needs to sleep means "My diaper is wet, and I'm worried what it will do to my baby-soft bottom. Change me, please."

It's a great thing to be able to communicate with another being without words. I can do it with my dog, who understands before I tell her when it's time to get in the bathtub, and when it's time to get her head out of the cat box. I can also do it with Adam. Just this weekend, for example, we were talking about the truck we're hoping to buy someday, and Adam mentioned that Lucy might eventually drive it to school. Each of us was silently pondering the "stick shift or automatic" question.

"Stop reading my mind," Adam hollered when I said it out loud. I obeyed, because he was also thinking dirty thoughts. Thoughts about meatball sandwiches with unholy amounts of cheese. But we do this all the time. It's one of the things that makes our marriage comfortable, like an old pair of jeans. Which reminds me how much I wish I fit into my old pairs of jeans. Anyway, when you know what someone else wants and needs before they have to tell you, and they know the same, it's a pretty comfortable thing.

It's also a handy thing, knowing what your child is thinking. My own mother put this to good use when I was a teenager. It was torture, actually, knowing that Mom used her powers to read my mind. But it kept me in line. For now, the mother's radar is keeping Lucy fed, diapered, and well rested. When the time comes, though, and she gets as bad as I was (but I hope, not as bad as her dad was), I will put this to good use.

I'll have to find something besides unbuttoning my shirt, though, to solve her most serious problems. No matter what the La Leche League says, there's a limit to how long that's going to fix things.

It Could Happen to You
How to Change a Diaper

For the next couple of years, Lucy will be a proud member of the Diaper Club. This is an exclusive group of individuals so privileged they get to throw away their undergarments— *sometimes after only having worn them for a few minutes.*

Not all members of the club deign to toss their unmentionables, of course. Some have highly skilled amateur launderers—even professionals—on hand for the washing. No matter how Diaper Club members handle their undies, though, they all have one thing in common: They dirty the diapers; everyone else does the dirty work.

Lucy has me attending to her Diaper Club needs around the clock. So, I have developed some rules to keep myself amused.

The First Rule of Diaper Club is that you don't talk about the Diaper Club. Wait a second. That's wrong. That was *Fight Club*. I guess I must be pretty tired to be confusing a movie with my baby's bottom. Or maybe it's common sense, telling me not to talk about poop. But I'm going to ignore that impulse. Lucy is a prolific diaper-dirtier, and the record should reflect it. Even though the books say she should only darken one diaper a day by now, she easily fills two, and sometimes as many as four. It is a consuming force in my life as a mother. Therefore, it's fair game.

The real first rule of diaper changing is to get someone else to do it. Fortunately for me, I have a very amiable husband,

and he is all too willing, even at two in the morning, to indulge me. I will almost certainly go to hell because of it. But it sure feels worth it now.

Usually, though, I have to break the first rule and change her all by myself, because Lucy and I are on our own all day long. And it's not that bad. As long as I remember to follow Diaper Club Rule Two: Wait for the poop.

Back when I was a really good parent, I would change her at the first sign of trouble. I'd stand up—not so easy, immediately after childbirth—and hustle her over to her changing table. I'd unfasten her little suit and carefully remove the diaper, so as not to disturb the icky stump of her umbilical cord. And then she'd poop some more. All over me, all over the changing table, and all over her outfit.

Now that I'm content to be an adequate parent, I wait until I'm pretty sure her tank is registering empty. Because Lucy is poetic, there are usually three telltale bleats that accompany a colon evacuation. When the third is heard, off to the changing table we go. It's not as if I wasn't warned about the river of poop, by the way. A friend who has a ten-week head start on me as a mother said it would happen. Another friend tells a story of the time her husband was changing their daughter's diaper. He bent over for a moment and barely missed being hit with projectile poop. I didn't want to believe it, just like I never wanted to imagine myself saying the poop word so many times in a single paragraph.

Rule Three is related: Watch out for impromptu pee. Sometimes, Lucy decides she prefers the free environment of her nursery to the confines of a diaper. As soon she's nude, she lets it flow and flow. I understand that with boy babies, this is even more the case. Now, I always put a cloth diaper down underneath, so that I don't have to wash the changing table cover a dozen times a day.

Rule Four is to remove Lucy's socks before starting the job. Babies are made of 80 percent water and 20 percent rubber. Most of this rubber lives in their legs, which bend and fold to such a degree that they can touch their dirty bits with their heels. Unless you want to wash socks with every changing, you learn to take them off. Even if it's a pain getting them on over those little peanut toes.

Rule Five is content management: Use the diaper to contain the toxic waste as much as possible. This conserves those precious wipes for blowouts that happen on the road, usually audibly, and in public places.

The sixth rule of diaper changing is to spend extra time on the ridges. Lucy's legs are like a stack of doughnuts. I don't know if it's baby fat, extra skin, or a side effect of the ridged potato chips I ate during pregnancy. But she's got more folds than a T-shirt display at the Gap. And things hide in there. Things that have no business touching a baby. It's not just her legs, either. I once found a bug wing in Lucy's neck. It was so gross, I wanted to turn myself in to the authorities in charge of child welfare. I have no clue how it got there, but at least I got it out quickly. I think.

The seventh rule is to know which way the diaper goes on. One side has Muppets on it and the other side has the flaps. For some reason, I could never remember which side went where, and I was forever wrestling Lucy's uncommonly strong legs twice to get the diaper under, through, and around.

Now that I've mastered the diaper change, I have realized this previously feared task is not that big of a deal, after all. It's also cosmic payback. I once wore diapers, and someday, Lucy will probably have to cater to a Diaper Club member of her own. I can only hope she's taking care of her own baby, though—and not her elderly mother.

Mother Love

There are many events in a girl's life that rarely measure up to the hype that precedes them. Take the sweet-sixteen birthday party, for example. What's that for? And how does life change afterward? All I remember about turning sixteen is that the entire swim team spanked me after practice, one by one. Few sixteen-year-old girls want that kind of attention directed toward their rear ends. And—what do you know—I wasn't one of them.

Then there's the senior prom. My date and I didn't know each other all that well, so it was an awkward, stiff evening. I shut my finger in his car door and quietly bled on my dress so that no one would know about it. He spent a good part of

the all-night party playing video games. All's well that ends
well; I think he's a lawyer now. But it wasn't exactly a
Cinderella evening. Mother Love has to rank right up there.
In fact, if I may abuse the expression, it is the Mother of All
Hyped Experiences. Given that, I'm no longer surprised or
ashamed of the performance anxiety about motherhood
before Lucy was born. It's a lot of pressure to feel the ultimate
love at the exact same time your lower half has split open.

And what if I didn't feel it? What if doves didn't wheel
overhead when Lucy emerged? What if angels didn't sing,
and—worst of all—what if I didn't think she was cute? Did
that mean I didn't love her and, therefore, wasn't a proper
Mom? I got a helpful piece of advice from someone who
already had children. "Don't expect to love them right away,"
she said. "It's okay if it takes a while."

Over time, I've come to understand this love a little better.
Yes, it's the desire to be part of the wave of hope, a wave that
represents each new life unfurled like so many yards of lace
on the rocky shore. It's the desire to see the life evolve slowly,
painfully, and beautifully over the years. But it's something
beyond that, something deeper and darker.

The day Lucy was born, I was so glad. She was healthy. I had
survived, and I was ready to get on with the real work of moth-
ering. I also thought she was incredibly beautiful at the time. I
marveled at how she had managed to be the only newborn
ever to emerge from her mother's loins without getting one of
those crazy baby heads. Now that I look at the pictures of her

first day, though, I have learned that mother love is blind. Lucy was beet red and her head looked like a Brazil nut.

Even after being bewitched by her at birth, I still didn't quite feel the pull of gravity I had heard described by the mothers who went before me. Rather, I was running on pure instinct, thinking only of protecting Lucy and of attending to her every need, responding to her every cry. I was so tired so often, I didn't feel much of anything at all.

Since then, something beyond this has opened inside of me. Every day I spend with her, it seems I have an experience so simple and joyous, I find myself in tears. Maybe in a few years, I'll look back and say, "Whoa! Hormones!" But for now, there's nothing like a new morning with her. Even mornings that follow one of those nights where Lucy does nothing but wiggle, kick, and eat, completely depriving me of the comfort of sleep, I still love the feeling of waking up with her. She's warm and fuzzy and more than a bit sleepy, and I hold her and nurse her until she passes out, drunk with milk. Eventually, she comes to, full of smiles and silliness. She loves it when I tap her chest and say, "You're Lucy." And I tap my chest and say, "I'm Mama." For whatever reason, this makes her giggle. And she giggles with her whole body. Her eyes crinkle and gleam, her legs kick, and her tongue pokes out of her mouth.

But even when she's not smiling, I'm finding myself living for the heft of her body and the curve of her china-doll mouth, set so perfectly between her moonbeam cheeks.

When I look at Lucy, it's like looking in a mirror. It's not that she looks like me. Rather, it's that I can stare as deep as I want, and I see eyes looking back at me just as deeply. Just as we sometimes look in mirrors to learn who we are, Lucy and I look at each other with wide, searching eyes, to better understand who is looking back. It's rare to look like this at another person. Usually, we worry about what that other person thinks of us. Whether we have salad in our teeth. And how dangerous it might be to let the feeling in our hearts glow through our eyes.

It's not that way with Lucy. The eyes gazing back at me are nothing but beautiful, and full of wonder and promise. I see this face every time I close my own eyes, and my heart tightens with the need I have for her. It's as though she's led me to the edge of a great, dark chasm, one so deep the bottom is invisible—if there even is one. My love runs that deep, and if anything were to happen to her, that's how far I would fall.

It's difficult, at times, living with that much to lose. But I can no longer imagine life any other way.

A Day in Cold Hell

Well, that's it. People need to stop what they're doing right this minute and have a sincere, sustained moment of pity, because Lucy has (dramatic pause) a cold. It's her first. Which means she'll get about seventy more before all's said and done, I suppose. But it also means she and I are todally bizerable here.

She caught it from me, so in addition to feeling like a wet sponge, I also feel guilty. I guess I was taking her perfect health for granted. Lucy managed to avoid the first cold I caught after she was born. It was a point of secret pride, I now admit. Lucy was so strong, I was fairly certain she would beat any cold virus coming her way. She was like a gladiator in a fat suit, flexing and lashing out against any and all microscopic invaders. I, on the other hand, was just a regular person in a fat suit, entirely susceptible to colds. Lucy's mighty immune system was going to appear in the record books. I just knew it. Nothing would take her down.

It didn't take long for me to be wrong on that count. Cold Number Two is a doozy. I gave it to Lucy, and Lucy has managed to infect my mom, Adam, and at least one sister. We're like a walking hot zone.

It was bad enough when only I had it. I had the chills, the sweats, the gloppy nose, and the unpaved throat. But when Lucy's chest started to rattle and her nose started to bubble, Adam and I fell apart. It was so tender and sweet when she buried her head into Adam's chest and wiped her snot on his shirt. And even more adorable is the whole-body-twitching prelude and delivery of a good sneeze: Even Lucy thinks it's pretty funny after she lets one fly.

But we didn't want to have any part in such cuteness. The idea of her suffering, even if it was just a little head cold, was about as appealing as a Jell-O salad with oysters. There was nothing to do, though, but give her a little squirt of baby cold medicine before bed. As she slept, she sounded like she was using an old saw on a piece of hickory. I was so worried about her I couldn't sleep myself.

It turns out I wasn't the only one. When 3 A.M. rolled around and I was starting to get delirious, seeing dancing lamb chops and the like, Adam woke up and took Lucy into her own room. He made himself stay awake and stand guard, because he was having the irrational kind of fear that only strikes after midnight: *Lucy won't be able to breathe if she closes her mouth.* I guess he figured his presence in the rocking chair would be the force that kept Lucy glued to the planet.

The next morning was something of a miracle. No, Lucy wasn't over her cold. There still is no cure for those, other than time, and not getting them in the first place. But she was hap-hap-happy—just like every other morning. She smiled and sawed hickory; she ate and sawed hickory; she talked to Adam and sawed a little more. And she wiped her nose on his shirt again. It was amazing. Here Lucy and I had the same cold. I had done nothing but crab, gripe, and wheedle for "bore tea." Lucy, on the other hand, at a mere eleven weeks of age, took her discomfort with astounding grace.

She was the same way after she got her first round of shots. She took five sticks in the thigh, cried for maybe a minute, then spent the rest of the afternoon chuckling like a maniac. And now, I'm here watching her play happily with her octopus toy, totally ignoring the little snail trail of snot under her nose.

I don't know yet if she's too good to be true, and will never complain about how miserable a fever is, and how annoying it is to have a stuffy nose and a cough. In so many ways, she already has been too good to be true. She's so beautiful and so beloved, that part of me wonders if I'm still delirious, even though I'm not currently seeing any lamb chops whatsoever.

But I wouldn't be at all surprised if finding happiness in bad circumstances is one of her skills. If that's the case, she inherited it straight from her father.

Time will tell if the art of suffering is something we learn as we grow up. And if Lucy learns it, well, I'm pretty sure I know where that talent came from.

Sniff, sniff.

A Taste of Baby Blues

Once when I was about ten years old, I did the most hilarious thing. I put salt in the little brown bowl we used to hold the sugar for our breakfast cereal. My health freak mom only bought unsweetened cereals, so it was up to us to fix that. It would be so funny, I thought, for whoever used the sugar next to get a nice salty bite of Cheerios.

The only problem was, I forgot I had done it, and I was the one who dumped a big spoonful of salt in my bowl. It was so awful. Just when I was expecting something nice and sweet, I got a big taste of Satan's armpit.

And this is what it felt like, one morning in the midst of all of this glorious new mother stuff, that I woke up feeling quite depressed. I had a heavy feeling, the ineffable gnawing in my head that something was wrong, and I really didn't feel like getting out of bed. I was overwhelmed with it. The mood wasn't particularly sudden. I'd had little flashes in the days before, little bruise-colored clouds slinking across an otherwise bright sky.

But that morning, I really felt low. And it scared me. I'd felt that way before and it was about the worst time in my life. When you're depressed, you forget that better times will come, and you tend to lose connection to the people in your life—people who can help you feel better. You can only think about how bad you feel, and how much you hate it.

Before I had Lucy, my occasional black days didn't really hurt anyone but me. I wasn't great company, that's for sure. But my dog, who was my main companion at the time, didn't mind. She took good care of me, in fact. And she kind of liked the fact that I spent a lot of time lying on the floor.

This time around, I had a baby who was utterly dependent on me for everything. Only one of us could wallow around helplessly, wanting to be carried everywhere and fed easily digested things. And it wasn't me.

Because I'd been through this before, I took care to read about postpartum depression before Lucy was born. I wanted to make sure that if it struck, I would be ready. Sometimes, it's easier to get through things when you anticipate they might happen. It's kind of like having the diaper bag of your psyche well stocked. You don't want to be caught in a crappy emotional spot without extra wipes, and maybe an entire change of clothes.

To tell the truth, I'm not sure if I was suffering the after-baby blues, or if it was just my own chemical makeup setting off little bombs in my mind again. It doesn't really matter, though. The fact is, I was unhappy. I felt all full of holes, shot through with despair. I needed to take care of it, if not for my sake, then for Lucy's. So, I reached into my psychic diaper bag. And thank God, there were no dirty diapers in there. Just things to help get me through.

For starters, I found some running shoes. I took Lucy outside for a good walk. Walking is not the same as running. It doesn't make me as strong, and I'm a far cry from the athlete I used to be. But getting moving is the first thing I need to do to feel better. And as much as I wanted to stay inside and rot in peace, I opened the door and went.

And I felt a little better.

The next thing the diaper bag held was Elaine. She would probably be horrified by the image of being inside a diaper bag. But hey, that's what friends are for. Elaine and I got together in my parents' giant kitchen for one of our regular industrial-cooking sessions.

Before we got started, I told Elaine that I was feeling pretty miserable—somewhat less happy than a lobster in a supermarket holding tank. I had cried for no reason at least three times that morning. It was awfully humbling. Elaine is one of those people who find the bright spots in everything. She's friendly, talented, organized, and extraordinarily generous. By comparison, I am a worm, accustomed to finding dirt wherever I look.

Elaine, bless her, didn't mind that I was moving in slow motion. She didn't mind that I could barely hold up my portion of the conversation. She just kept encouraging me and gave me permission not to make the tuna casserole we had planned, as well.

By the time the day with Elaine was over, I still didn't feel great. But we had made a freezer full of chicken enchiladas, mashed potatoes, and lasagna. And I'd rather be miserable with a full freezer than with an empty one.

Later that night, when Adam got home from work, I confessed how I was feeling to him. This was hard. Adam never gets melancholy. He almost never gets angry. And he's almost always smiling. Sometimes, I hate being the bruised apple in the family basket. Those are the times when I wonder what Adam gets out of this deal.

But I asked him for help, anyway. And he gave it, in his kind, systematic way. "What's the one thing that has you most worried?" he asked.

And I told him. It was a writing project I really wanted to finish, but couldn't seem to find the time to do. "Okay," he told me. "You're not doing anything on Saturday until that project is done. I'll take care of Lucy."

"And then what?" he asked.

I went down the list. I was worried about what to do about going back to work. Whether we were going to have enough money if I didn't. Whether I was repulsively fat and unlovable. The list went on. When I talked about these things one by one with Adam, they started to shrink back to their proper size, instead of clotting together as one tangled mass in my mind.

Now that I have a few weeks' distance on that day, I'm getting some important perspective on this new life I'm living. No matter how happy I am to be taking care of Lucy, there may well be some bad days and dark moods that come out of nowhere and threaten to kick my feet out from under me. And I can't look to Lucy for the cure, no matter how cute she is. A baby doesn't stand a chance against the complex chemicals and circumstances that conspire to make a person feel bad. What's more, she needs me to take care of her, not to feed off her emotionally. She also needs me to take care of myself, so that I can give her all the time and love she requires to thrive.

Not only am I too old to be doing things like putting salt in the sugar bowl, I am old enough to know how to ask for help when I need it.

They say it takes a village to raise a child. I'm not sure that's exactly it. Right now, I feel like it's taking a village to raise me. My brothers and sisters and in-laws have all taken turns holding the baby on too many occasions to count. Even the ones who don't live in town have taken a whole lot of time to love me long distance. And even on the worst days, I know I'm lucky to have parents who will let me mess up their kitchen. I'm blessed to have friends who'll mess it up with me even if I'm not a laugh riot that day. I'm fortunate to have a husband who's patient enough to talk about the things that make me afraid.

Most of all, I'm lucky to have a reason to do all of this: a baby who needs a loving and healthy mother. Most things we do in life don't really matter. At work, for example, no matter what we do, we can always be replaced. Things might not be the same. But they will go on.

It's not that way when you have a child. Life changes. You take the bitter with the sweet, but most of all, you keep going. And there's no going back. You do what it takes to raise that baby well. A life—her life—depends on it.

Chapter 7

Good Times and Guilt

Mothers, food, love, and career: the four major guilt groups.
—Cathy Guisewite

There's a fifth group: your children.

I've Found My Inner Martha

People say they hate Martha Stewart. But I think that most people—most women, anyway—have a secret desire to be that handy and creative around the house. It's as though we're those Russian nesting dolls, and each smaller doll within represents a secret dream of something we'd really like to be, a dream hidden behind the lacquered exterior we offer the world.

Some people have sex kitten dolls, some have Mother Teresas; others have swinging corporate raider dolls or little athletes in painted-on jogging bras. And lots of women—more than would admit—are secretly harboring little Martha Stewart dolls, dressed in Oxford-cloth shirts and slacks, and maybe an overpriced pair of gardening clogs.

My inner Martha Stewart doll is the center one, all stubby and small and deeply buried because the truth is, it's really hard to be Martha Stewart.

Taking time off from work after you have a baby is a wondrous opportunity to unscrew your inner dolls and spread them throughout your mental house. You pick up your little Martha Stewart and think, "Hey, lady. You're taking care of a family now. You really should do it right. With linen napkins, homemade bread, and perhaps a small, simple quilt for baby."

After a few minutes of this nonsense, you say, "Screw the linen napkins." And then, "The bakery up the street makes really good bread."

The dream of making something for baby remains, though. In my case, I dreamed of making new couch pillows for Lucy. Yes, I know that babies do not actually yearn for new couch pillows of their own. And I also know that some mothers have a bad tendency to project their own dreams onto their children. Think of it this way: Lucy needed new couch pillows as a favor, not a present. She ruined the original couch pillows by spewing milk curds all over them, and she really thought replacing them was the right thing to do, only she's been a little short of cash lately. And wallets. And pockets to hold them in. Diapers and leggings have their limits, you know. And people just don't pay babies what they used to.

In addition to the milk incidents, there was also a big diaper blowout, but we didn't tell Daddy about that one, because it happened to the pillow on his chair. Besides, the pillows are already poop-colored, so it's not like anyone would have noticed. And she really did mean to replace them, so why belabor the issue?

So, as a favor for Lucy, I signed up for a sewing class. I already had a machine that Adam bought me for Christmas two years ago, when I was a newlywed and I first cracked open my inner identity dolls and found that little Martha Stewart, with a pair of sharp shears and a bolt of fine Irish muslin. I put the sewing machine in the closet after the cunning little velvet wine bags I had planned to make as gifts came out crooked and thready. And I put Martha Stewart back into the bigger, more sensible doll she came out of.

It took me a while to get to the first class. For one thing, I had deep-seated insecurities that started in the 1970s, when I took my first sewing class and needed Mom to rip out every seam I made and put in a straight one. The quilt I cut out in college didn't help. Its pieces are still sitting in a bag somewhere, no doubt resenting me. And the wine bag incident is pain, fresh pain. Martha Stewart is just lucky I didn't give her to the dog to chew on.

And then Lucy and I got colds, and I had writing deadlines, and I also needed to devote adequate time to beating up on myself because I wasn't getting in daily workouts at the club on top of the hill. Self-flagellation burns almost as many calories per hour as walking, but is often followed by snacking, and generally is not a good way to shed baby fat. But this is the one kind of daily workout I have the discipline to do, so what can I say?

Finally, though, I managed to make it to a Monday night sewing class. I pumped a nice little bottle of milk for Lucy and met Adam at my parents' house, which is close to where he works and close to the sewing school. I also brought some formula, in case Lucy downed the bottle of milk and was still hungry.

The class was two and a half hours long, which would be the longest I've been apart from her, and I wanted to make sure she'd be okay. I fed her right up until the minute I left and put her down—all sleepy and warm—in the portable crib.

"This is perfect," I thought. *"A little time to myself, a little productive adventure."*

Apparently, by the time I got to the stop sign at the end of the street, Lucy was up—and angry. I, on the other hand, was calmly driving to class, thinking about pillows. Tassels or fringe? Perhaps a festive button in the center?

Meanwhile, Adam and my sister, who traveled to my folks' house to help, managed to soothe Lucy with a toy for a few minutes. This was probably just enough time for me to get to the class and meet Vera, the lovely woman who was going to teach me the secret of pillows. While Vera and I chatted and flipped through the manual (the sewing machine knows sixteen different languages! *Mein Gott!*), Lucy cried and cried. While I learned to thread the machine, and took a few test runs down a swatch of fabric, Adam and Susan heated up the little bottle of milk.

Adam says he didn't tell Susan it was breast milk, and wonders if she would have been splashing big test drops on her wrist if she knew. While I adjusted the tension of my thread, Lucy tried drinking from a bottle for the first time. And then she used her newly skilled hands to push it away. While I was learning all about the rotary cutter, and how to avoid slicing off parts of my fingers using this convenient device, Adam was holding the now furious Lucy, who was screaming at the milk gods who'd forsaken her in her hour of need.

Apparently, she was screaming loud enough that the guardian angel on my shoulder heard, because Vera and I pretty soon ran out of stuff to talk about, and I didn't have all the material I needed to make pillows anyway. So, prompted by these unseen forces, I went back to my parents' house—a good half hour early. As soon as I got out of the car, I heard this terrible sound—kind of like an old blender trying to chop ice. The front door flew open and my brother ran out and said, "I think Lucy needs you."

I trotted inside and found her in my sister's arms, making a tremendous amount of noise for such a small creature. And when I picked Lucy up, her face got this look on it—I imagine it's the same wild-eyed look lost dogs get when they find their way home. I rushed her over to a chair and started to feed her. She felt like an industrial-sized vacuum cleaner honing in on a pile of grit, and she held on with both hands and didn't let go for a good forty minutes.

By the time we got home that night, Lucy had forgotten all about the trauma of being separated from her own, private cow. She actually squealed with delight in the elevator going up to our condo. It's an ugly, ugly elevator, lined with stainless steel, but Lucy is at a stage where she loves shiny things.

"Yes, shiny!" I said to Lucy, as she held tight to my jacket and made parakeet noises. *"Shiny!"*

Lucy was in a fine mood for the rest of the evening. She played and chirped, she giggled, she blasted poop through her outfit. And I realized a little something. A little something besides the fact that Lucy is going to need to learn to drink from a bottle.

That little Martha Stewart doll wasn't Martha Stewart, after all. And she wasn't holding scissors. Rather, she was holding a baby, and loving it, and not so sure she would ever be able to let go. For now, I'm glad I don't have to. And I'm glad that Lucy's holding on to me as tightly as I'm holding on to her.

Even if it means I've got some pretty gross pillows in the living room.

We're Bad Parents. Really Bad

Last night I counted. Lucy has been liberated from the womb for fifteen weeks. And for nearly every week she's been with us, Adam and I have done something that clinches our victory in the World's Stupidest Parents contest. I know we're not the only parents who screw up. It wouldn't be much of a contest if we were, now, would it?

We're *way* ahead of Russ and Elaine, and their daughter is two months older. All they've done is clip Morgan's finger instead of her fingernail. And once she fell out of bed. And another time, Elaine forgot to buckle her in her car seat when they went out for a drive. But it doesn't make me feel all that much better. I have scored so many points in this contest I am working on my "You hate me. You really hate me" acceptance speech.

Let's start with the time when Lucy was five weeks old. I was trying to put her into the swing and Adam called and, while I was explaining to him just how much Lucy had cried that day, I broke off half my fingernail in the swing fastener. Since I had totally rid my system of any traces of the delicious epidural block, this little mishap smarted. A lot. And it startled me so much that the phone squirted out from its nook between my shoulder and ear and bonked Lucy. Right on her head. She already was antiswing at this point in her life, and this was just the excuse she needed to let me know, once and for all, that she would not be taking a little ride that afternoon. And instead, she would require some more holding and a lot more milk. If she felt like it, she might even gum me really hard. And I was not to complain.

And I didn't complain, most likely because the swing incident occurred on the very same day I bent her leg backward when I was flipping her over to the other side to nurse. It was horrible. I looked down there to see why she wasn't quite connecting, and I saw her foot had been transported unnaturally up to her butt. She must have seen it too, because pretty quickly, she shrieked like a burning monkey.

I vowed I would never tell a soul what I had done, because I didn't want anyone to turn me over to the authorities. But in the months since, Lucy has done a good deal of kicking and standing, so I'm feeling pretty okay about it—I guess in the same way that robbers can't resist bragging about their unpunished deeds. I do have my passport ready for a life on the run, though. This is because in the weeks since, Adam and I have done all sorts of other things that make us look at each other, turn pale, and shudder.

One morning, for example, our living room was kind of cold. So Adam put a hat on Lucy. We left it on for her morning nap, and later found her in her crib, wailing, because the hat, made out of a loose knit, was covering her face. She looked like that Dumb Donald kid on Fat Albert, only her hat didn't have a giant breathing hole.

And this isn't the only clothing disaster.

I took a walk one chilly day up the hill to the bakery. It's about a mile away, and somewhere between home and the bakery, Lucy lost her socks. Both of them. People had been looking at me a little more than usual, and I assumed it was because they were admiring my exceptionally beautiful child and resenting me for my good fortune. Or wondering how someone who looks like me could have such a beautiful baby.

As it turns out, they were staring at her feet, which, while still lovely, were also blue. I didn't notice for blocks and blocks. Not till I put my hand down to squeeze one of them. *"Dang!"* I thought. *"She lost a sock."*

And then, about a minute later, *"Crap! She's lost both socks!"*

I didn't have any spares with me, so all I could do was keep her feet in my hands to keep them warm. This wasn't easy, considering I had the dog on the leash. When I got to the bakery, I considered buying a pair of French rolls, hollowing them out and slipping her feet into them. But if she couldn't keep socks on, I didn't think she'd do too well with baked goods. And I didn't want to call any more attention to the situation. Any time you make a fashion statement with food— even if it's French—this tends to be the case.

I devised a way to wrap my coat around her feet for the return trip, as my hands were full of leash and bread. And she didn't lose any toes to frostbite, but her feet were practically purple by the time we were home.

Of course, frozen toes are better than being coyote bait. Adam and I spent a recent afternoon tromping around a muddy field in the country. We took pictures, planted trees, and forgot all about our city-slicker problems. Only thing is, on this one particular day, Adam forgot more than just his problems. He came strolling through the grass with a camera.

"Where's Lucy?" I said, when he got close enough.

"Um, on the porch," he answered.

The porch was only about, oh, a hundred yards away. In other words, ninety-nine yards farther than I normally tolerate. It's not unusual to see eagles, owls, and coyotes out there, carrying off any number of rabbit-sized delicacies. Compared to Lucy, even a weakling rabbit is an elite fighting machine.

Quietly and calmly, I said, *"Adam, you *$*&*#%$! Coyotes could get her!"*

We ran back. She was perfectly safe, but Adam wasn't. I'm sure he wished he had a tranquilizer gun—and not to use on the coyotes.

Other incidents have been less glamorous. Adam once bonked her head on the gate of our hatchback car after an on-the-road diaper change. And on numerous occasions, I have put her down for "tummy time" right after a feeding. This is a really good way to ensure your baby gets to play with a face full of puke. And she lets you know what a gay time she is having by crying and screaming so hard the curtains rip in two.

By far, though, the worst thing we have done is let her watch the Teletubbies on TV. She loves them. And while her cold toes, bumped head, and bent legs have recovered, I think Teletubby damage is permanent.

When she's forty-three years old and starts squealing with

glee when something shiny appears in front of her, I know who gets the blame.

PBS.

Okay, that's not true. I'll blame Adam. That is, if I'm still here—and haven't been packed away to the prison for incompetent mothers. I sure hope Lucy will come for a visit—at least once in a while.

Lucy in the Sky with Diapers

Sometimes, the unsolicited advice people give struggling mothers like me is actually good. People told us, for example, that four-month-old infants make excellent travelers. And since Lucy was brushing up against this milestone right around Thanksgiving, we thought, "What better thing to do than fly to Cincinnati for the holiday, then off to New York for a little fun on the second busiest travel day of the year?"

This all seemed like a good idea up until the day before we left. And then, the full realization that I would be trapped in an airplane seat with a possibly screaming Lucy for hours and hours started to make me feel sick. Not airsickness-bag sick, though I am always comforted by the fact that airlines provide those little niceties, even as they cut back on in-flight peanuts and fruit garnish to shore up their profit margins.

But all that worrying, it turned out, was for nothing. Lucy is a champion traveler. She loved the foldable plastic cards explaining what to do in case of sudden loss of cabin pressure, although she didn't realize that's what they were talking about, because Adam made up an entirely different story to go with them.

"These people are really tired, Lucy. That's why they're bending forward and crossing their arms in front of their faces. And see this daddy breathing into a balloon? He thinks it's so much fun, he's giving one to his son. But not before he breathes into his first. And this lady is very excited to be going down this inflatable yellow slide."

Lucy also enjoyed the airplane food—probably because it's the same breast milk she eats on the ground. I didn't want her ears to hurt during takeoff, so I fed her and fed her. And then I fed her some more. Lucy probably ate for an hour straight. It was an eating orgy for her, and it produced dramatic results. It was as if a little gastric diva had decided to make a grand entrance, a very grand entrance, once we hit our cruising altitude. I knew just how grand an entrance it was, because I was holding her.

So, I suggested to Adam that perhaps he might like to change her diaper. This was horribly unfair of me, because he had changed her last diaper in the waiting room at the airport. And while Lucy was nude, she took the opportunity to start peeing. And she peed and laughed, and peed and laughed. Adam picked her up to get her out of the puddle, which made her laugh and pee some more. She laughed so hard she started swinging from side to side. She was a peeing pendulum at gate B5. And there went her first outfit of the day.

Nonetheless, I was fairly certain Adam would enjoy the challenge more than I would. It was a man's challenge. An engineering and plumbing issue, with a little bit of physics on the side. Besides, I was in the window seat.

And so to the lavatory they went, Adam toting Lucy and the diaper arsenal, and Lucy toting a suit full of poop. Minutes passed. And then more minutes. People began lining up in the aisle outside the lavatory, shifting and looking irritable. But the OCCUPIED sign remained lit. Yet more time passed, and I started to wonder if perhaps something was wrong. I kept popping my head over the seat and staring back at the angry throng waiting, and no doubt thinking someone should have brought his Metamucil. Finally, though, they emerged. Lucy was in an entirely new ensemble, which could only mean one thing: a three-layer blowout.

"Note to self," I said to my thumb. "Next time, also bring a change of clothes for Adam." He was looking like he needed one.

"How did it go?" I asked.

"It was like being inside a coffin," Adam said, describing how he had to undress her, wipe her, and rediaper and redress her, without putting her down. Lucy had poop up to her neck. He had to clean her and the lavatory, which should give people planning to join the Mile High Club in a Delta MD-80 a reason to think twice about it.

"Thank God I had a Hefty bag," he said. "I am officially broken in as a father."

Meanwhile, Lucy enjoyed being inside the coffin. It was well lit and full of shiny metal, which she loves.

A while later, we touched down at the Cincinnati airport. Adam's parents were waiting for us in their usual spot. And just as we reached them, I felt a low rumbling emanate from Lucy's backside. She had gone again. And this time, for sure, it was my turn.

Uptown Girl

Not long after Adam and I got married, we started to look for a house. We wanted something with a porch and a yard. Nothing fancy, but something with a view of more than the neighbor's garage. And hopefully, something cheap.

After touring house after tiny house, including one harboring a giant, stinky python, we realized that we had far better taste than we could afford, and that it would be better for us to buy some property in the hinterlands, and eventually, build something dreamy. After all, when we someday—in a long, long time—had children, they would be able to play in the dappled shade of oak trees. They would be able to catch frogs, plant a pea patch, and learn how the innocent look of a deer is actually a cunning mask hiding the evil-tree-eating, horned slug within.

So, we bought a beautiful piece of property that we later learned is a giant, government-protected swamp. And then we learned that we can't afford to build a house there yet, although a garden shed is well within our grasp. Still, we're pleased as could be to have our own park where we don't have to pick up dog logs, and where we someday will squeeze juice from apples that grow on the trees we planted when we were young and peppy, and hadn't heard of leaf curl, apple scab, or fruit blight.

Naturally, Lucy—who arrived long before we thought we'd be parents—has let us know that she loves cities. Especially big, expensive, crowded cities, like New York. After our trip to Ohio, where Lucy went antiquing, saw lights at the zoo, and played with her cousins, we took her to the Big Apple, figuring if we could make it there, we could make it anywhere.

My friend Nan, who will someday be a widely read author, but for now is a young and glamorous writer with a cool apartment in Greenwich Village, was kind enough to put us up. She used to have a dog, also named Lucy, who occasionally peed on her bed, so I guess she figured nothing worse than that could have happened. There is something worse that could have happened, but it didn't.

We walked all around the West Village, Soho, and the East Village. Lucy was delighted. We toured Midtown, Chinatown, and Rockefeller Plaza. We visited Central Park, and ate through a United Nations' worth of ethnic food. "Bravo!" Lucy said to all of it, more or less, but especially to Vincent van Gogh's *Starry Night* at the Museum of Modern Art.

Frighteningly, however, Bergdorf Goodman might have been Lucy's favorite place. Because she needed a diaper change, I headed first for the ultraluxurious ladies' lounge. Once freshened, Lucy and I walked through the baby clothes department, and decided that perhaps a college education would be a wiser and cheaper investment. And then we came upon the most wonderful sight of all: the Christmas rooms.

In the very center of them stood a huge tree laden with glittering ornaments that could only be called fabulous. Lucy started cooing and shrieking when she saw them, so much so that the woman from the fine jewelry department stopped and said, "I'll show you a quarter-of-a-million-dollar diamond, baby."

So that we could dodge the risk of Lucy ingesting the quarter-million-dollar keepsake, we passed on that opportunity. Instead, Nan and I waved ornaments over Lucy's head. The one that made her squeal loudest, we decided, would be her New York souvenir. Who knew there was such a thing as a Christmas ornament that cost $36?

Well, now I know. But Adam had it wrapped in a beautiful, silver box with a lush, red ribbon, and it will forever remind me of our trip.

It'll also remind me of something else: It doesn't matter what you dream for your child. Even if it's something as pure and shining as the idea of summer evenings spent dodging gnat clouds and hunting for chorus frogs, your kids decide for themselves what it is they truly love, and how it is they will someday live.

Even if we want Lucy to grow up with mud up to her elbows, and knowing the taste of an apple straight from the tree, she may decide that she's a city girl at heart, that a Big Apple is the better prize. And that the first chance she gets, she'll be flying far, far away to make her way in a steel and glass forest utterly different from the one she grew up in.

Every year, when I take that sparkling ornament out of its box, it will be a year closer to the time I'll lose Lucy to the world, and wherever her passions take her.

Even now, though, I know she made a beautiful choice.

The Ever-Changing Baby Face

I had a revelation after we got home from our trip: Lucy's clothes are not all made out of horrible cheap cotton, shrinking and shrinking by the minute. On the contrary, she's growing. Those little pants that were baggy on her just two weeks ago are now starting to look like something a well-dressed baby would wear to a flood. And that achy feeling I get in my arms after I've carried her for a while isn't a sign that perhaps I have an angry biceps cancer that will end my life in months. Rather, it's a sign that Lucy is getting heavy.

At four months, she weighs fifteen pounds—nearly twice

the weight she was when we first met. But this is the weird thing about the way babies grow. She looks exactly the same to me as the moment she was born. When I look at pictures, of course, I can really see the difference. Lucy's day-old legs looked kind of like the sticks my dog picks up at the park, a little bit thin and scaly, but totally lovable. Now, they look like big rolls of bagel dough. They're smooth and rubbery, and impossible not to squeeze. In the alien invasion, I'm sure babies will be considered a great delicacy. They're that delicious to behold.

These rapid changes get me thinking that unless I write down the things about Lucy that really touch my heart, I will forget about them. And she'll someday be thirty-five years old, with a full set of teeth, and I won't remember how much I love the tiny ribbon of gums that shows when she's really, really smiling.

My uncle told me that I'd always see Lucy's baby face in front of me, even when she's grown up. And I hope this is true. But I want to see *all* of the faces Lucy ever wears during her life, all at the same time. I want to remember all of the changes, especially because they happen so quickly.

It's not that I have a favorite version of Lucy—at least, not yet. Whatever size she happens to be always feels like the perfect size. I think this is why I haven't been able to perceive her growth, except through pictures: Even though she changes constantly, I wouldn't change a thing about her.

When she was very tiny, I liked how her whole body fit in my lap. I could lay her down on my legs and cradle her in my forearms, and we could have entire conversations.

"Do you like me better than you like your daddy?" I would ask. And then I would make her head nod up and down.

"Do you think Daddy should do some laundry?"

Lucy would always agree. Now, though, she no longer fits there. But she fits perfectly between my elbow and shoulder when I hold her like a ventriloquist holds his dummy. Which makes me realize there is a whole new routine waiting, if I can only learn to throw my voice.

I think I will have her say, "Daddy, run out and get us some nice Chinese takeout." Or maybe, "Daddy, don't you think Mommy's shoulders could use a nice rub?" How can he resist?

And it's not just the way Lucy fits in my arms that makes me swoon. I love the bald spot on the back of her head. It started out as a stripe, which left her with a little mushroom cap of hair on top. She looked like a monk. But since she's gained neck control, she mostly looks up, and now, her stripe has widened in the middle so that it looks like a giant, toothless grin. She kind of looks the same, coming and going.

I also love her feet, especially the way her toes curl down when I touch them, like a grabby little monkey.

I love the way she keeps her mouth open when she's trying to talk, even between words. She may never say the letter *m* unless she grows out of this.

I love her tiny fingernails.

I love how she arches her back now to let me know when she wants out of the crib.

I love how she laughs after she sneezes, and how she hides her face when she sees another baby—even the one in the mirror.

I love the way all we have to do to get her to smile is wave our hands and bark like dogs. And how, when she's in her carrier, she kicks her legs and shrieks like a mynah bird when she sees something she really likes.

And the "Yuck, brussels sprouts" face she makes when we put a little teething medicine on her gums.

And especially the way she clings to us when she's waking up from a nap, like a soft scrap of cloth fresh from the dryer.

I've come to realize that I will probably think Lucy is perfect at whatever size she is. But there is the possibility that her adorable quotient is shaped like a mountain. It will peak. And after that, she'll just get less and less cute.

And if that happens, I'll look at her and say, "Well, Lucy. What do you know? You were cuter yesterday. We can hope for a turnaround tomorrow, but I wouldn't hold your breath."

I'm not going to hold my breath either, though. Because I can't imagine that day will ever come.

My Breast Friends

It's a good thing I love Lucy so much, or I'd be embarrassed she's seen me without a shirt on so many times. I have never been particular friends with my breasts, probably because they've made such a half-assed attempt to be present in my life. When I was a freshman in high school, for example, one of my teachers was trying to give an example of how certain names often have stereotypes that go with them.

"Take the name Martha," he said. "What qualities do you think of when you hear the name Martha?"

"Flat-chested?" offered a boy named David.

"Not quite what I was thinking," the teacher said. "What about dark-haired? Studious? Sincere?"

Much like, "My, she has pretty eyes," means nothing *but* her eyes are pretty, studious, and sincere are synonyms for flat-chested. This is just one reason I did not love high school.

I had decided long before Lucy was born that, flat or no, I would definitely nurse her. I found some very good reasons to do this: Not only do breast-fed children have slightly higher IQs, they also get immune-system boosts.

But as good as these reasons are, I'm not sure they're good enough to have kept me nursing her these last several months. Rather, these are my on-paper reasons. They're the kind of statements you can float out like pretty balloons when well-meaning strangers look at your pregnant belly and ask if you're planning to bottle- or breast-feed.

If I looked into my soul, though, I would probably find that the real driving force behind breast feeding Lucy is that it keeps me from having to wash bottles. It also spares me the hassle of packing formula in the diaper bag. And it's free. Free and easy offer immediate benefits—the kind of thing that gets a sleep-deprived mother through the day a lot more easily than the promise of IQ hikes and enhanced immunity. And then there is the not-so-little matter of weight loss. Someone once told me that breast feeding is also a good way to accomplish this.

Finally, there's that old saying that there's no better way to bond with a baby than to feed her milk from your very own jugs. This may well be true. But I know plenty of people who've adopted babies, and plenty of fathers who, try as they might, have failed to lactate. And from what I can tell, they have bonded beautifully with their children.

That said, nursing Lucy has been a really great experience. I'm pretty sure we've bonded because of it. When she lifts up my shirt in public, for example, I do not scold her, or even blush. I just think, *"Boy, she's getting really good at grabbing, isn't she?"*

And when she barks with joy while I'm unhooking the goods from one of these high-tech nursing bras, I just think, *"I know, Lucy—I am a very good cook!"*

I also really like the new trick she performs while eating, where she raises one hand like a flag, and rests it against my neck, palm facing out. I can't resist sticking my finger in her hand, and she grabs on and yanks it up and down. This amuses us both.

There are some challenges, though. Since she was born, I estimate I have fed Lucy nearly two thousand times. She's one of those babies who early on liked to eat just about every hour. And, since Adam and I failed utterly to get her used to a bottle, my presence was required for all of those feedings. It still is.

The frequent nursing sessions are exhausting. But more often, they are just messy. At my dad's seventieth birthday party, when Lucy was only a week old, I had to move really quickly to keep a rogue fountain of milk from spraying into another guest's salad plate. And I still leak through shirts regularly, which can get a little cold in the middle of winter.

And even though Lucy loves breast feeding, I'm not sure other people love it when she does. I recently had dinner with a good friend of mine who has had his armpits sniffed for *Time* magazine, where he writes a humor column. But armpit-sniffing and breast feeding are not in the same league, apparently, because Joel nearly passed out when Lucy ducked under the table for a drink. He later sent Lucy a little velvet hat, so I'm pretty sure he's over the trauma. Still, though, a lot of people just aren't used to the act.

Take my eight-year-old niece, Emily. When she first met Lucy, she loved everything about her. And she had questions about everything—especially the eating part.

"Does that hurt?" she asked, craning down for a better look.

"Why is your pimple so big?" she said, once she got her peek.

"You mean my nipple?" I said.

"Yeah, that."

I wasn't really sure, so I just said it fit better in Lucy's mouth that way. But she had made an intelligent observation. You do get kind of enlarged down there when you're nursing. When my milk first came in, I suddenly was enormous. I had the kind of chest I always dreamed of having, the kind I could mimic by putting two pairs of tube socks in my little trainer bra.

"My God!" I hollered to Adam when I noticed what had happened below my neck. "I look like a freak!"

A slow, curious grin spread across Adam's face when he saw what I was talking about. Adam, who always makes me feel beautiful, and has never once complained about my studious and dark-haired look, only had one comment—something I never thought I'd hear anyone but Lucy say:

"Can I touch them?"

Solid Food, Solid Sleep

My sister-in-law Jennie has a great talent for summarizing the world in a way that is succinct, truthful, and often quite funny. "You have to remember that sleep deprivation is a form of torture," she told me when Lucy was a few weeks old. At the time, my sweet little baby was waking up every hour and a half during the night, and I was so tired, I was practically incoherent.

Like Linus with his security blanket, I've carried Jennie's insight with me in the months since. It's made me feel better countless times to realize that, even though I was having a hard time taking daily showers, I was as tough as a soldier, and had the body odor to prove it.

For example, in an attempt to have an adult conversation with Adam about an article I had read, I said *"Yew Norker"* instead of *"New Yorker."* For five months now, I've had trouble with consonants and vowels. And don't even get me started on the diphthongs. But then last week, something amazing happened. Lucy slept for six hours. And then she did it again. And again, and again.

The first time it happened, Adam and I were a mess. Three A.M. rolled around, and both of us were wide awake. Our eyes were like quarters we were so wired. Why, we wondered, was Lucy still asleep? After confirming that she wasn't dead, we did the only sensible thing: We watched a Conan O'Brien rerun. It was a little weird watching him sing Christmas carols with Tom Hanks after Christmas, but it was definitely better than that infomercial featuring the extremely scary face-exercising hockey mask.

The second time it happened, we had gone to sleep at nine P.M., and I was the happiest person in the world to be wakened at three for a feeding. After the third and fourth times, I was practically levitating.

Vowels, consonants, diphthongs, the elusive schwa sound, and even entire words that had abandoned me during baby boot camp flooded back, as did my ability to fold laundry. Before, and much to the chagrin of my neatnik sister Susan, I had been merely *bending* my clothes.

I don't know why, when Lucy turned five months old, she magically started to string together hours of sleep, like so many lustrous pearls on a fine silk strand. But I'm thinking the reason could be linked to Lucy's consumption of solid food.

Although you never get a straight answer from the baby books, people like my mother-in-law swear that solid foods make babies sleep longer at night. From the time Lucy was five weeks old, Carol has urged us to give Lucy just a few spoon-fuls at night. But we didn't start until Lucy started getting interested in our food—and until my dad had started giving Lucy little tastes of ice cream. This is something grandfathers do, and despite all the stern looks you can muster, there is no way to prevent it. So, you might as well just give up, like I did, and let her dig her little paws into your dessert. And then you feel extremely guilty, break out the rice cereal, and hope she hasn't developed a permanent aversion to anything resembling nutrition.

The thing is, though, Lucy hated rice cereal.

The first time she ate it, she got this sad look on her face. Her lower lip went slack, and all the cereal slid slowly down her chin. She gets sincerity points for this. We were sure to take lots of pictures. She tolerated two more bowls over the next couple of days, and then let us know that this rice cereal thing was not going to happen.

Elaine suggested mixing it with a little banana. So we tried that. "This is beyond disgusting," Lucy said, only not in so many words.

Adam developed a theory that Lucy had grown to fear the spoon, because it had come to her so many times bearing the detested rice cereal. So, he started feeding Lucy straight banana goo off his finger—another thing the baby books say you shouldn't do. But worrying about that after she'd already eaten multiple forms of ice cream is kind of like worrying about the Chiclets you stole just before torching the grocery store.

We were starting to get pathetic. Not only was all this solid food not helping her sleep, she wasn't actually eating as much as she was squishing food around in her mouth so that it would ooze more smoothly down her chin, behind her ears and—I have no idea how—above her left eyebrow.

But feeling pathetic is the mother of desperation. Desperation leads to shopping, which led to us buying a box of baby oatmeal. And miraculously, Lucy ate it. Though both look like paste, oat paste apparently tastes better than rice paste. Even twice a day.

After two weeks on this routine, she started to sleep. We will never know for sure if the two things were related, because Lucy just isn't telling. But, I suppose, it doesn't really matter. The important thing is: This spoon-savvy infant is very close to sleeping through the night.

I thought neither the age of spoon nor sleep would come. When she was first born, the pressures of feeding her felt endless. She always wanted food. It was often exhausting, especially during the long hours before dawn. I felt like I was treading water in a whirlpool. But now, with a little perspective, I am reminded of a line from *Zorba the Greek*, where he is asked if he is married.

"Am I not a man?" he replies. "Of course I've been married. Wife, house, kids, everything . . . the full catastrophe!"

Before I had Lucy, I would have thought so many sleepless nights signified catastrophe. Shattered slumber for months on end would have meant something was terribly wrong, that I was ruined, the unluckiest person in the world, and probably dying.

But instead, with Lucy, I feel I am among the luckiest. Night after choppy night, what has kept me afloat is the sight of her impossibly tiny, perfect body lying in bed between Adam and me, where she slept for her first few months. Her round face looked angelic: perfect, pure, painted silver by the light of the moon. As those days are coming to an end, I'm realizing how much I will miss them, and what a blessed thing it is to have my life interrupted, to embrace the full catastrophe. I don't know if I'll ever see anything as beautiful again in my life as the face of my sleeping child beside me.

And I don't know if there will ever be anything as difficult that I will love so much.

The Great-Baby Clothes Debate

If you think having a baby will bring you and your husband closer together, you're only partially right. Adam and I are now closer than ever. We're so close, we touch, which is a shame considering I do not always have time to bathe. We have to be this close, to get around the ton of baby paraphernalia in the condo: the sparkling music arch, the crinkle mats, the red-and-black gym thing, the plastic chair of rainbow fun, and the ten thousand cloth diapers positioned strategically throughout the apartment in case Lucy decides to puke.

Close as we now are, I am finding out all sorts of things about Adam that make him different from me—things I never noticed before now. Things that make me say, Hmmm.

They mostly have to do with clothes. I never noticed it before, because Adam always looks great to me. But the man has *no idea* how to put together an outfit. He's been riding my shopping coattails now for years. His clothes more or less match because we buy them in all the same colors, usually at the Gap, which is also known as Garanimals for grown-ups.

Now that Lucy is here, I am finding out just how difficult this fashion thing is for Adam. This is not his fault. Adam grew up wearing tube socks, which do nothing to prepare a man for the cruel fashion world. They don't even have a heel and a toe, and I'm pretty sure he never learned the difference. So it's no wonder he is having trouble with the baby.

Adam really likes to dress Lucy in the morning. I love this, because it gives me a little more time to sleep. But it does mean that I often have to fix his little fashion faux pas. For example, he sometimes puts Lucy's socks on inside out. What few people realize is, socks really hate this. In the sock world, being inside out is like flashing your heinie when you bend over. It's terribly embarrassing. I could tell this mystified Adam, who also flashes his heinie when he bends over.

Another time, Adam put Lucy's pants on backward. And this is how our talk about that one went:

"Adam," I said. "Do you see these little built-in feet? It's important that the toes point forward, because that's the direction Lucy's toes point, and as her parents, we should do what we can to keep it that way."

And then there was the time Adam failed to match Lucy's blanket with her outfit. We had left the apartment without bundling her fully, and Adam gallantly raced back upstairs to get something nice and warm. He came down with a pink-striped blanket, which simply did not match her red hat.

"Adam," I said. "If I had gone upstairs, I would have chosen the blanket with the red flowers. That would have matched much better."

We even have blankets that have *exactly* the same pattern as specific outfits. His own mother bought them for us. But it doesn't occur to Adam to use those items together.

What it all comes down to is this: It never occurs to Adam that clothes are anything more than a barrier against the elements. The poor man has no idea that there is a higher power than Mother Nature. And that is Mother. Mothers understand the power of the ensemble, and the rules that go into creating one.

When there is an outfit that consists of pants with bunnies and a matching jacket, it is disturbing to the mother to see the bunny pants next to the T-shirt with the sheep on it. Bunnies and sheep do not fraternize; they each keep to their own portion of the meadow. Is it so hard, then, to match the species on Lucy's top and bottom?

I tell you, I still would have married Adam if I had known he was this cavalier about blankets, socks, and appliquéd animals. But I might have included a line in our prenuptial agreement—right below the one about me cleaning toilets and Adam cleaning cat boxes—that said he was to respect the separation of species on clothing.

Frankly, though, it never occurred to me that I would face this monumental challenge. I'm pretty sure our marriage is strong enough to take it. But come school picture day, I'm in charge.

Adam responds

Little green army men do not wear tights.

When I was a kid, playing with dolls never once required that I dress them. Naturally, I had hundreds of those green army men. They were already dressed in clothes—army green—that exactly matched their army green helmets, weapons, and skin.

I also had about a dozen Lego men. The firemen wore red stripes, just like my tube socks, which were also quite fashionable at the time. And the police were decorated in blue stripes, just like my other tube socks.

I had plastic dinosaurs, which I never once tried to fit into jammies. I never had to color coordinate my Hot Wheels. I never once had to debate the right heel height for Mr. Potato Head's shoes. And my Micronauts were already painted in the appropriate colors, as seen on TV every Saturday morning.

Had Lucy come into this world painted, like the dolls and toys of my youth, none of this would be an issue.

But she arrived naked, just like the books said she would. And so, I've had to learn how to dress her. First, one thing to make clear: I thoroughly enjoy dressing baby. That's because, for whatever baby-only-knows reason, Lucy loves the changing table. Unless she's really uncomfortable or terribly hungry, changing time means several uninterrupted minutes of smiles and giggles.

One day, though, I came out of the nursery to show Martha how dang cute she was—something that we both do for each other with embarrassing frequency. Martha looked at Lucy, then at me, then at Lucy again. And she had a look on her face that could only be described as "I love you, Adam, but you're a total idiot."

"What?" I asked.

And then I learned that, in the dimly lit chaos and clamor of the changing room, I had put one of Lucy's socks on inside out. It wasn't long before Martha said under her breath, "Arrrgggh," and fixed the so-called problem.

As I watched her change the sock so those frightful seams were hidden from public view, I sarcastically wondered, "Does the sock work better that way?" To me, the purpose of the sock is to keep the foot warm. Backward, schmackward. When the toes are pink instead of blue, all is right with the world.

Later, it became clear to me, as it had already to Martha, that we simply had different points of view about baby clothes.

See, some people get a baby dressed. Others dress baby.

I'm a person who gets the baby dressed. That means the thought process involved can be described in two-word sentences made of gruntable words. "*Feet cold. Need socks. Socks on. Unggh.*"

It's all about necessity. It's all about fulfilling needs and creating order in the world. It's all about making sure that the little green army man with the machine gun is in front of the guy with binoculars, not behind him.

Martha, on the other hand, is a person who dresses baby. The thought process is more complex and requires clauses and phrases and sometimes-careful timing.

"*Do I have socks to go with this outfit? The pink socks are dirty, and I don't have time to wash them, so I'm going to have to change her shirt.*"

It's about detail. It's about going the extra mile, beyond simply creating order toward creating an impressive image.

After all, we've taken more than a thousand pictures of Lucy—mostly after Martha has dressed her so her outfits match the blanket she's lying on, and both are optimized to look good next to the furniture, and inspirational when bathed in whatever sort of sunlight is available that day.

That's not to say I haven't been simply stumped by some of the baby clothes. I have no idea who thought tights for babies was a good idea, although Martha insists they keep her warm and they don't fall off. I know this has been a source of trauma for her.

But it took me twenty minutes to get those stretchy little suckers over Lucy's legs the first time I tried, and I still had to call in for reinforcements. And there was one outfit—some sort of pastel-colored tunic wraparound thing with ribbons for ties—that to this day I can't figure out. Clothes for baby should not be inspired by the ancient art of origami.

The bottom line is this: My role as new father is to be overly concerned about the welfare of the baby. I'm like Lucy's one-man Secret Service, ready to jump in front of assassin's bullets and protestor's cream pies. If the baby is cold, I'm going to put her in something warm. If the baby is going outside, I will put on a hat to block the sun. If the baby is wet, I am going to put on something dry.

Let's face it. I will never see clothes as anything but shields against the elements. Martha, on the other hand, sees them as little pieces of art. It's going to have to be Martha's job to teach her the rule about white shoes after Valentine's Day, or before

Arbor Day, or whatever the deal is with that. Martha will have to keep Lucy from becoming a Fashion Don't.

The fact is, one day Lucy will be able to dress herself. I'm going to miss the privilege of putting her pants on backward. But I hope she accepts the gift of tube socks. That's an article of clothing that has my complete respect.

Why I Quit My Job

While I learn all about Adam's tube-sock hang-up, I am learning equally important things about myself. And this is why I am not at work today, even though I'm supposed to be. Something happened as the date for my return to the office drew nearer: I realized there was no way I could be apart from Lucy all day long.

Perhaps I should have seen this coming. Growing up, I used to sleep in bed with all of my stuffed animals, because I was afraid some would get hurt feelings if they were banished to the floor. And once I got Misty, we went nearly everywhere together.

The first year I had her, I was a high school teacher, and I brought her to class. She would occasionally help herself to the delicious sandwiches in brown bags that sprouted like mushrooms in the hallways, which meant I was always shelling out lunch money to the students she robbed. But it was a good life, even if we were poor and Misty was fat.

Once I started working in less dog-friendly offices, I started dropping her off at my parents' house every morning so that she would have quality day care. And of course, she joined Adam and me on our honeymoon.

But by the time Lucy was born, I finally had a job I loved, and I was working with a group of people I respected. And Misty was a happy, well-adjusted dog who would only occasionally binge on cat poop. So, I figured this day care thing could work. I would find an excellent caregiver for my human child, and instead of just dropping off Misty for day care, I'd deliver Lucy, too.

What I really wanted to do was find a nanny, preferably Mary Poppins. That way, Lucy would have someone devoted to her needs all day long. It's not that I think day cares are bad because children generally only get divided attention there. Any stay-at-home mom with more than one child faces that problem. And there are some really great day cares out there. But Lucy couldn't even sit up on her own, and I didn't want to imagine her stuck on the floor, in need of some attention, and having to wait even a second for it.

It's one thing for her to have to wait for me, as she sometimes does when I'm putting clothes in the dryer or dishes in the dishwasher. Irrational as it is, it just feels worse to have someone else treat your child as you might. And not just because you have to pay them to do it. It's like when you were a kid and you heard another kid say something mean about your brother: You can say whatever you want, but anyone else who tries gets a punch in the nose.

I started my nanny search on the Internet so that I wouldn't have to have any scary human contact early on. That way, I could learn all I needed, without having to let anyone know I was a total naïve. Also, I didn't want Lucy to hear. She doesn't talk yet, but you never know what she understands and doesn't. For all we know, babies play dumb because it takes time to form a perfect parental manipulation strategy. Once their plan is formed, they're free to start talking. I'm pretty sure that's what Lucy is doing all day. She's already quite good at working me over, and that's even without saying "Mama," "need," or "sparkly tube top."

Anyway, the nanny-search sites proved to be a fine place to start. While I am sure there are many excellent caregivers there, I managed to find all the flakes immediately. My favorite was the one who said she "didn't believe in discipline, only positive redirection of negative inclinations." The sentiment is nice, of course, and something I'm mostly on board with, but I still didn't like the sound of someone clapping her incense-scented hands together and saying, "Lucy, I salute your interest in that hot stove. But might I interest you in something a little cooler? The refrigerator, perhaps?"

Also, it's shocking how many of these nannies are only eighteen or nineteen years old. I am far enough from that age to think it's very young, and near enough to remember the things I did then. And that's what has me fully freaked out by the prospect of letting someone like I was near my child. When I was nineteen, it was pretty much all the effort I could muster to wash my jeans once every five wearings, and my sheets once a month. Making my bed was something I did to find the nickels to trade for the quarters that would help me afford the Laundromat. For food, I ate curly fries, coffee, and the occasional bagel. I know. It's gross. I'm disgusting. But I was known as the clean freak in my dorm because I showered daily. So you see the influence I was under.

It is obviously unfair to judge all nineteen-year-olds by my own past. Many women that age are excellent mothers themselves. In fact, I know one of them. She is amazing and mature in ways I never was. But I just couldn't see myself handing Lucy over to a stranger with fry breath and foul jeans, even if those things are only in my imagination. So, I called my mom, the nurse. What better person to beg for support than someone who not only is sanitary, but also will know what to do for a scraped knee or case of cooties? What's more, she loves Lucy.

Mom was willing to take care of Lucy on her day off. I couldn't think of anything better than this, except for staying home myself to take care of baby. But I put that thought out of my head, because I felt a duty to return to work—my team was counting on me, I liked my job, and we needed the money to straighten Lucy's teeth, and maybe send her to college. My boss was willing to let me work part time—say, three days a week, and one of those from home. This meant I had to find someone to care for Lucy only one day per week. For that one day, I thought, I could trust her to another pair of hands.

And so every morning when I woke up, I told myself, "Today will be the day you find a nanny." But I kept finding reasons that made this task impossible. Lucy's feet needed kissing. She was hungry and needed to nurse. Her cheeks needed a little baby lotion, because they kept getting chapped on our walks. Or, I had something I needed to write for a deadline somewhere.

Days, then weeks, went by, and Lucy had no nanny. And as I usually do when there is a task I keep putting off, I stopped to think for a minute about what was really going on. That minute turned into hours, and then days, while I thought about what I had been doing with my life, and how it compared to the life I thought I would have when I was small.

Back then, I had big dreams. I would be a writer, I thought. And write I did—little-girl short stories that were long on humor but short on form. As I grew up, I dreamed of chuffing down America's highways in a pickup, with my dog by my side. We'd devour the red-painted skies, beaten copper lakes, and whiskery evergreens framed by the mouth of our windshield. The sights would sustain us because there was no way we'd make any money doing this.

My wise and well-meaning parents advised me to have something to fall back on, just in case. And because I am more or less a good daughter who didn't think she deserved any special luck anyway, I did just that. From the Monday after I got my college diploma to just a few weeks ago, I had been devoted to my career. I taught. I worked at a newspaper. I built Web sites, then managed teams that did this. And then I became the editor of one of the world's most popular Web sites—one that had more than ten million readers a day. Considering that I was falling back, I was doing a pretty good job of landing in higher and softer places each time.

And I loved the journey. No, I was not doing what I always set out to do. But life isn't about doing what you thought you'd be doing, and getting what you thought you'd get.

Or is it?

To be honest, I never saw myself wearing elbow-length poop gloves while hunched over a grinning, gummy baby who is thrilled with the trumpeting flurry that has come out of her peach-shaped bottom. And I never thought I would find that sort of thing to be hilarious. Or that I would love that little lump of wiggly, messy flesh so much.

Sometimes, though, life hands you just the lesson you need. If I really wanted to be a writer, then that's what I should have spent my time doing—not worrying about failure and ensuring it completely by building a career doing other things.

That's one of the funny things about having a child. Just as you have started to understand the value of time, your own supply runs out. Suddenly, and for the rest of your life, you will no longer be able to follow a dream with your body and your soul. There is no packing up the pickup truck and hitting the highways with a soda and a sandwich. That's because there is a baby who needs you. A baby who will become a child who will become a teenager who will become an adult leaping off into her own future, reaching for her own dreams. And by then, many years will have separated you from the vision you started out with—so many that it's possible there are not enough years left to get back to that clean, bright place where it all began.

Seeing this is where wisdom begins, and you realize you don't need all the time in the world: You just need to make the time you have count.

Writing is hard. Writing with a baby is like writing, but without the convenience of two hands. Often, the best I can do is to hold her in one arm while I peck away with the other. While the quiet click of hobbled typing delights her, I find myself thrilled by the beating of her heart, which I can feel with my free hand. It's a tiny knock-knock, like an acorn bouncing across a stone courtyard, counting out seconds, symbolizing life, and reminding me that whatever comes, I'm finally traveling the right path.

Chapter 8

More Than We Can Chew

Mistakes are part of the dues one pays for a full life.
—Sophia Loren

I thought I was done paying dues when I quit the Girl Scouts.

The Tooth Hurts

I am a little obsessed with teeth. This is not just a recent thing. It predates Lucy, even. Ever since I found out that Adam had to have every one of his permanent teeth removed to make room for the extra set that was coming in behind them, I have carried a small, hard pellet of fear in my heart. Add that to the fact that I teethed at four months and was a something of a biter—and suddenly, I had enough fodder to fuel a fair amount of worry.

Imagine the baby, I thought, who would be born with not one, but two rows of teeth. Hucksters of yore would have sold tickets to see *The Amazing Shark Baby, Live!* It didn't happen. As soon as Lucy's four-month birthday rolled around, though, I started looking for signs of imminent teething. Drool, crying, frantic gumming—all of these were sure indications to me that Shark Baby was on her way.

Since then, there has been a lot of drool, and a fair amount of crying, sometimes even at the same time. But these have been nothing compared to the gumming. Gumming has become Lucy's day job. No matter what else she is doing— bathing, playing, holding my hand, reading, nursing—she finds a way to let her gums in on the fun. Everything goes into her mouth for a good chomp. Books, magazines, her feet, her finger, and occasionally her thumb, not to mention remote controls, dog toys, the corners of her high chair. *Everything.*

It has only gotten worse since she learned to scoot and wriggle around on the floor, not unlike a potato bug suddenly exposed to daylight. She has even humped her way to such filthy things as cast-off shoes. I found her once trying to gnaw the corner of my "walk the baby fat off" hiking boot. There's nothing quite like a dirty boot in your baby's mouth to prove once and for all that you're a terrible housekeeper. But, as I'll say to the judge, that's not entirely my fault.

When you're living in a two-bedroom condominium, and using your dining "nook" as a combination home office and playroom, sundries are bound to pile up. And pile up they did: cloth diapers for toxic leaks, shiny plastic toys, rattles, books, Beanie Babies, orphaned socks, videotapes, coupons that I will never use, receipts that I meant to file. The list was endless. These things threatened to bury us in a time capsule of mostly well-intended consumerism, and for once, I am not exaggerating. Much, anyway.

The only bright side was that they had turned the condo into a human-sized Habitrail, and I was getting in very good shape meandering through them, with or without my fat-burning shoes. I was logging about a mile a day between the bedroom and kitchen, mainly because I had to take so many detours around all the baby stuff. Looking back on it, it is not surprising that Christmas was the last straw for the condo. We emerged from the holiday season with so many gifts for Lucy that one last wee hat set off the crap alarm, which bleated like a lamb until Adam and I made the decision to sell our condo and buy a house.

That took less than two weeks. Normal people spend a lot more time on this process. But Adam and I belong to the Band-Aid Removal School of Life Events: best they should be dispensed with quickly. And within two more weeks, we were in the house. The greatest house in the world, as far as I am concerned. It's a 1905 Craftsman with—and this makes my eyes smart—a kitchen large enough to house Lucy's high chair, the dog bowls, the cat bowls, with enough room left over that Adam and I can both stare at the microwave while it makes us our dinner.

Still, moving is hell. And two days after we moved in, Lucy and I caught colds. Two days after that, Lucy turned six months old. Far from enjoying a momentous event, we spent her birthday and the days surrounding it listening to Lucy shriek. And not her usual "I'm talking with dolphins" squeal. With that one, it's clear she's trying to communicate complex ideas. What they are, we do not know. But they are nuanced and shaded, and they rarely break glass.

Her six-month shriek, on the other hand, was something else. It said one thing: "I'm in pain." Adam and I thought she must have a horribly stuffy head. We could hear the snot rattling in her nose, and she wasn't sleeping well at night at all. For me, the only bright side was that I could take the noise for hours on end, without considering child abandonment for even a millisecond.

Too bad I'm too much of a dope to have figured out what the problem was. Otherwise, I could have prevented the shriek in the first place. Adam and I had been quick with the gum-numbing goo two months earlier, when we didn't need it. But by the time she had an actual tooth coming in, we didn't do a thing. I guess I could say the distraction of having to put all our earthly possessions into small cardboard boxes, tape them shut, then cut them open and unpack them caused me to miss the fact that a small, diamond-sharp tooth was on its way.

But the truth is that the novelty of teething had already

worn off weeks before. I had thought so much about it that I simply ran out of mental juice for this event. It was the developmental milestone that cried wolf, I guess, and by the time the signs had arrived, I had stopped looking for them. So, it was a great surprise for me to stick my finger in Lucy's mouth and feel something ridged and hard attached in there.

"By gum!" I exclaimed, more or less accurately. "It's a tooth!"

It was just a tiny one, a speck of white, like rice for Barbie. But I had to tell everyone, or at least their answering machines, I was so excited. I never would have thought something so small and ordinary as a tooth could fling me into orbit. And I can't believe I almost missed it. That's the thing about having a baby, though. It's a chance to watch life open up before you, like a time-lapse film strip of a flower going from bud to blossom. You get that strange sensation of moments passing quickly and slowly, all at once. With your own baby, you get to feel these changes, and not just see them. You have to pay attention, though, and not just think about all the unfolded laundry and unpaid bills. The threshold moments help you understand a little bit better what it means to be human, and to be alive.

To touch life like this, to feel it bloom in front of you—this is the only kind of magic that is real.

A Guy's Guide to Baby Holding

Another one by Adam

I am not an athlete. Never have been.

When I was very young, for example, I played T-ball. That's the baseball game where they put the ball on a post instead of using a pitcher so really little kids can actually hit the thing.

In the history of T-ball, I am the only kid who has struck out. And I did it twice.

When I retired from baseball, I chose to play goalie in youth soccer because I was too lazy to run as much as the other kids. I gave up a lot of goals that year, since I have a policy of not standing in front of a speeding soccer ball, let alone throwing myself in front of one.

In junior high, I went to athletic camp, where I excelled in things like "crafts" and "archery." At least archery was a good choice socially, since Robin Hood made it one of the few nonathletic activities that's still considered cool by other kids.

I was also on the worst intramural high school basketball team to have ever played in my hometown. We never won a single game, nor even came close. My endurance probably had something to do with it. I learned a couple of years ago that I can run about two miles before it starts to feel like my kneecap has a nail in it.

In other words, I'm basically one of the short-of-breath weaklings who couldn't toss a medicine ball more than once without pulling something.

So, it is with more than just a little physical agony that I have learned to cope with my sixteen-pound, always-needs-to-be-carried baby. All I can say is, whoever came up with "bundle of joy" must have been as strong as a mule, or the parent of a wafer-thin baby. I would have chosen "load of joy."

As I write this, Lucy is nearing the six-month mark, and is just over sixteen pounds. She's nearly as heavy as she's ever going to be before she can move around without my help. Yes, crawling is imminent for Lucy, but until then, it's in my arms (or Martha's) every waking moment.

I will relish the day when Lucy wants her sippy cup, and she is able to toddle over to wherever it is herself, without requiring any intervention from my biceps, my triceps, my deltoids, my not curiously strong altoids, my thyroid, and most of all, my back.

But until then, I have to content myself with a few things. First, I'm definitely a bit stronger than I was. And second, something equally valuable, I've learned coping mechanisms for holding my hefty load of joy.

I realized this the other day as I watched one of my best friends, who is expecting a baby in March. He was trying to hold Lucy the way I used to, by holding onto her rib cage with one hand under each armpit—the same way you would hold a bowling ball just before dropping it off a building.

My friend was clearly not comfortable, and Lucy—as sincere as ever—shifted her gaze at me, lifted a lip in a certain way, and let me know that I was to fix this problem or else there'd be hollering.

So, in a quick motion, I showed my friend the two-hooks technique. One arm hooks under her bottom, like a little bench, and the other arm hooks around her chest, just underneath her wee armpits. This way, baby gets to look forward just like before, but can now lean against your chest, which makes her feel a bit lighter, and also puts the strain on one bicep instead of two, which means with some careful switching, you can hold her that way a lot longer. It's a great party hold. My friend made the change, and Lucy's lip went back to drooling as usual.

I was the recipient of similar information, not long ago. My brother-in-law (father of three) relieved me of holding Lucy one day. He flipped her horizontally, put her chest on one of his forearms with her head near his elbow, and let her arms and legs dangle on each side. We call this the Leopard Hold, since it's what a big cat looks like when it's lolling on a tree branch.

When you're holding Lucy this way, her weight feels like it's been cut in half. And more than that, she loves it, since with just a little effort, you can rock her in great big smile-shaped arcs. This makes her laugh and laugh, with an occasional birdlike squeal that startles the cats.

The motion a particular hold allows is equally as important as the hold itself, I've learned. The two-hooks, for example, is excellent for the soothing up-and-down bounce, but useless for swinging, which is only a good idea when baby feels like playing.

I also learned that babies can sense fear. If you're stiff and worried, the baby will be also. Half the challenge is just relaxing.

But here's the most important thing I now know: When it's your baby, it's not how big your biceps get, or how good you are at developing new, innovative, and possibly patentable holds.

Holding baby is, for some reason, something that makes me proud to be a father, and proud of myself. Changing diapers is *not* on the list, no matter what Martha may write, the sneak. It turns out that there is something about the way I prop Lucy in my right arm, or sling her over my left shoulder, or lay her across my arm in a Leopard Hold, that's just *better* in Lucy's mind than all the other guys in the world.

When I cradle her after a nap, she curls up in my arms like a turtle still hiding in its shell. When I hold her when she's mad, she grabs my shirt with both hands and pulls me toward her so she can yell at me louder. And when I hold her in front of a mirror, she smiles so hard she just melts into my chest. And when she starts crying, sometimes I can just hold her, and she'll stop and maybe even go to sleep, right there on my shoulder.

And when she does that, something happens to me that has never happened before. Lucy feels as light as a feather and I am, without a doubt, the strongest guy in the world.

Back in the Running

Adam might not be an athlete, but I am. Or at least, I was, until I got pregnant and couldn't break a sweat without getting sick to my stomach. For a long time, I wondered if I ever would feel fit again. And then, not too long ago, as I was nearing the end of a five-mile run, I realized something: I wasn't tired. In fact, I thought I could speed up a bit. And so I did, marveling at my strength, my form, and the incredible day it was turning out to be.

Not long after that, I heard a woman huffing hard and closing the gap between us. Though I would rather be passed by a strapping young man, preferably with winged heels, I didn't mind being beaten by another woman. I didn't mind much, anyway. And I figured this young goddess was lean and fit. A modern Atalanta. Probably a college athlete, preparing for an important competition. Good for her.

Then I heard a rapid little thwap-thwap accompanying the heavy breathing. Thwap-thwap-thwap-thwap-thwap-thwap, it went. Thwap-thwap. Curious, I turned around to see the source of this strange noise. I saw a pair of tiny dogs pulling not a college athlete, but a woman easily ten years older than I am. The dogs' little gnome faces looked like they were laughing at me. And soon, their little gnome buttocks were over the horizon, mooning me rudely.

Thus ended my fantasy of being completely back in shape. It was only a fantasy, after all. You don't get *Baywatch* fit by only running and lifting weights a few times a week. Doing more with Lucy has proved to be very tough. There are so many things to fold into the day: household chores, writing deadlines, doctor's appointments, dog walks, grocery store trips. And this does not begin to take into account all the extra invitations I get to do fun things because I'm no longer "working."

Before Lucy, I could take care of the business of living whenever I wanted, which created the illusion of more time. Really, it was just that I had more control. Life after Lucy, on the other hand, is a balancing act. There are the unscheduled inevitabilities that have to get taken care of right away—things like wet diapers, worse diapers, and heart-felt melt-downs when she's really tired. And then there are the things I want to do, or need to do to preserve my sanity. If I don't do them when I have a free five minutes, they'll never get done. Perpetual motion is the key, although directed physical activity—like a nice, leisurely run—is a luxury.

Given that, I decided to be very happy I could power through a five-mile run. So what if I was slower than the world's teeniest dogs? I was running once again. I had taken on the challenge of pregnancy, and I survived.

Lots of women wonder what having a baby will do to their bodies. Though it varies from woman to woman, pregnancy will almost certainly never become a fad beauty treatment. It can be the fast track to Dumpytown, what with all the puking, the stretch marks, the water retention, and the good old-fashioned fat, euphemistically called maternal reserves. The few people who actually do look and feel good during pregnancy perpetuate it as the ultimate physical experience for women. That's such hogwash. Being pregnant is really hard, even without complications like gestational diabetes or bed rest.

But before I had Lucy, I was counting on living the myth. And I rounded it out with some extra fantasies of the vainest nature. For example, I read that nursing burned so much fat, many mothers actually emerged from the experience thinner than when they started. Because I knew I would be having children at some point in the near future, I let myself invest in some maternal reserves before actually conceiving. Lots of people prepare for childbirth by readying the nursery or creating a will. I ate my way to the starting line. Those extra pounds would come right off, right?

The way I was planning it, my two-liter-bottle abs would shrink into a six-pack within, oh, four weeks. What's more, I was certain I would finally get that pair of sculpted arms I'd always wanted. I'd be carrying the baby around all day. What else could be the result? Linda Hamilton from *The Terminator* was my role model here. In *T1*, she was a little doughy. Just like me. In *T2*, after she had her baby, she was totally buff. Never mind the fact she was also locked in an insane asylum and dodging a liquid metal robot bent on killing her. She had really, really great arms.

What *actually* happened was that I was left with both

It Could Happen to You

maternal and paternal reserves. In addition to this, I had canine and feline reserves, lodged in my neck and stomach as though they had signed a long-term lease on the space. Because of this, I deeply regret my decision to wear a horizontally striped stretch top to a party the week after Lucy was born. The pictures will live on forever, and my stomach and arms are stretching those stripes so I look like I'm wearing a topographic map of Mount Everest.

Six months and a few weeks later, I am finally able to wear an acceptable size of pants again. Note that I did not say my regular size. I am not there yet, and not certain that I ever will be. Draining those maternal reserves is harder than they say. They seem to be an unlimited natural resource. It's too bad you can't heat a house or run a car with them. That's all right, though. I have Lucy. I am back in shape. And I've learned a thing or two about what it means to have a baby.

A lot of people say it's the ultimate physical experience for a woman. This is hooey, because it sends the message that once you've had a child, you've already done the best thing you can do with your body. And that's not really true. Yes, it's a miracle that we can give birth. But the real miracle is the life that emerges, not the experience of being pregnant. If you're lucky, like me, you get to experience it. But once you've conceived a child, it's not a daily challenge to transform the cells into another human being. It just happens. It's tiring, to be sure. And you have a responsibility to eat the right foods and avoid unhealthy things. Whether you like it or not, though, that baby is going to be born. You can't skip a day of pregnancy like you can skip a workout.

And this is why there are lots of other physical experiences that can have just as much meaning as having a baby. They're the experiences that require the courage and self-love to dream, and the dedication to do them. In this way, it's amazing to be able to run a marathon. After my first one, I cried, and not because of the pain. When you experience something like this, your spirit feels bigger than what your body can contain. It is pure joy to have a body that does what you want it to do. The miracle is finding the discipline and strength to challenge it every day, or at least every chance you get. These are the moments that remind you you're alive.

If there is a secret to living well, and to being the person you want to be, it is in realizing that you have power, and you have choices. It takes courage to do things that are difficult. It's easy to find reasons why you can't. But if you look at every moment as an opportunity, you're halfway there.

One of my favorite quotes, by Goethe, is "Do not hurry; do not rest."

And this pretty much sums up the way you balance having a child with having a life.

When you have a baby, you trade your nice, orderly life for one that is chaos and kisses. You can't hurry, because babies have schedules of their own. You can't rest, for the very same reason. If you're ever going to be the person you dream of being, you learn to seize the moments you're given. You don't plan for the life you want to have. You live it, as best as you can. And even if you're not going fast, it still feels like you've taken flight.

Two Plus One Equals Enough

Lucy is now seven months old. Back when I measured her life in days and weeks, I couldn't imagine we'd ever make it to this point. It's not that I worried that the world was coming to an end, or that I'd misplace her along with many pairs of her very small socks. Rather, it was that I was living from minute to minute, and day to day.

You know what they say: "Take it one day at a time." It's supposed to be encouraging. Like all you have to do is make it through one day, and you're home free.

The thing is, people with newborns aren't thinking about tomorrow, or any future more distant than the next diaper change. For all you know, this is the rest of your life. It sure feels that way. One day contains one-thousand four-hundred and forty minutes. And you feel every one tick by.

But like the skin slipping off a chameleon, those days eventually do pass leaving something larger than you imagined in their wake. You find yourself the mother of a shiny, medium-sized baby. One with quick smiles, bright eyes, and the incredibly endearing habit of holding her arms out to you every time you come anywhere near her.

Lucy has two bottom teeth now, sitting side by side like barnacles. She can sit up by herself, though she tips when she's distracted. She is in love with the dog and thinks the cats are pretty swell, too. And she's not just eating oatmeal anymore. Her favorite food is peas, with chicken 'n' dumpling puree coming in second by a carrot. Her guilty pleasure is to drink from an adult's water glass. Her favorite letter is *B*, if one can judge by the frequency with which she says Bah Bah Bah. She bites everything from the phone to furniture legs. Her greatest innovation is "froggy voice," the croaky rumble she makes with the back of her throat. Her new laugh, "The Muttley," has entertained people from New York to Alaska. It sounds like heavy breathing, but without all the sexy baggage.

I am careful to note these small things because I have learned that today's baby is not the same as the baby of yesterday or last month. Already, I can feel her infancy slipping away. Now that the bruising first few months have passed, I can imagine Lucy turning one. I can picture her as a two-year-old on a red tricycle. I'm ready for her to take painting classes at the art school down the street, and they don't even teach children younger than age six. I know I'm going to miss the seven-month-old I have, but I am already crazy about the seven-year-old she will become.

The one thing I cannot conceive—and I mean that in every sense—is another child. It would kill me, I swear. So, this is why I am especially stunned to realize that when I was Lucy's age, my little brother Andy was on his way. And when my mother was the age that I am now, she already had four kids, and was working on the fifth.

It's not that I'm ruling out the idea of ever having another baby. It's just that I can't yet imagine doing it again with a toddler hugging my shin, let alone one on each limb. It's like entering a pie-eating contest right after vacuuming up a ten-course meal. No matter how much you love pie, there's only so much one person can take on a full stomach. I don't want to think about how parents of twins do it.

I do envy them one thing, though: They don't have to make the choice whether to give their child a brother or sister. And as impossible as it is to imagine doing this all over again, a part of me knows I just might. And I have several great reasons for it.

The first is my older brother John. He and his wife, Kim, who looks curiously like me but is a much kinder person, live in Chicago, so we don't get to see them as much as we want. When were little, I admired John so much I used to wear his underwear. In my defense, I was only three. We fought plenty. But he was—and is—a good brother. In third grade, for example, I won a big spelling bee. I'll never forget the moment Mom came to pick us up at school. Even though John had lost his grade's bee, he grabbed my hand and stuck it in the air when he saw Mom's car. He had the grace to celebrate my victory. And I don't see any irony in the fact that the word he spelled wrong was maudlin. It's a nice story, for crying out loud.

Andy is my younger brother, and the one I used to hug in preschool every morning when he was having his routine cry.

You might cry, too, if a fish tank fell on your head while you were climbing up the bookshelf. During a vacation from his very grueling job last year, he told me he was going to bring "a few rhododendrons" over to our country acres. He swiped fifty plants from my dad, who is a rhododendron hybridizer, and he planted them all. Unbelievably, mine is not the only garden he has adopted.

Ann is reason Number Three. She's the one who bakes all our birthday cakes. And she looks after Lucy on Saturday mornings so I have more time to write, and so Adam has time to do chores around the house. She's also the first of us to become a parent—she's a stepmom to an incredible nine-year-old named Katy, whose father, Michael, is one of the smartest people I've ever met. He also makes a mean cup of coffee. Despite these fine acts, and her good choice of mate, Ann's crowning achievement is the time she made coffee come out of John's nose at dinner, just by saying, "Nar." She's that funny.

And then there is Susan, who is last only in birth order. I named her, because my parents had run out of energy for such things, and this makes me feel a special sort of account-ability for her existence. Susan lives only a couple blocks from me, and has been an incredible support during these hard months. She's the reason I can run long distances again, and the reason I can fit into most of my old pants. Her level head humbles me. We had an earthquake here recently, and during it, Susan and Lucy were upstairs together. When the house started rocking, I was frantic for Lucy, though I knew running upstairs was the wrong thing to do. I stood in the doorway, struck dumb by fear. Susan had the presence of mind to call down during that long forty-second ride to let me know Lucy was okay. She turned a natural disaster into just another Wednesday.

But it doesn't take anything as dramatic as an earthquake to remind me how much I love these guys. I think about it every day, especially now. Growing up, they taught me empathy and justice. They taught me to care more about someone else's successes and failures than I cared about my own, and how to love someone else more than I love myself.

When I think about it, I realize this is the kind of love you need to know to be a good parent. And so for this reason, and this reason alone, I think I might someday have a brother or sister for Lucy. I want her to know this feeling, before she even knows how to ride a bicycle.

But not yet. She's about to crawl. And something tells me when that happens, I'm going to be taking it one day at a time—all over again.

I Love Lucy and She Loves Me

All mothers have grand plans for their babies. Especially their first babies. The ones who name their children Keanu, for example, are planning to raise stiff little boys who will become major action stars with excellent teeth. The ones who buy the

Baby Einstein video are hoping to raise physicists. My aspiration was more humble, sort of: I hoped to teach Lucy to swim before she was six months old.

I have reasons for this, and at least one of them is good. My parents live on the water, and so it's a matter of safety. Also, Lucy's aunts and uncles were excellent swimmers, so she might have some talent. And even if she isn't Olympic caliber, her feet resemble flippers. It would be a shame not to at least *try* them in the water. And for the good reason: I bought her a really cute little pink tankini in the three- to six-month size.

With this in mind, I found a book about teaching infants to swim. We practiced in the tub. Then, when she was two months old, and unfortunately too small for the tankini, I slipped her into a swimming diaper and took her to a really warm pool. She seemed to enjoy herself. Though she was not an experienced smiler back then, she definitely beamed as I tugged her chubby body through the water. At the time, she was mostly head and stomach—two parts that float great. What that says about her head, I do not know. But she was pretty much a cork, bobbing away in my hands.

That was all well enough until I had to change her out of her swimming diaper and back into her street clothes. I understand the economics of why locker rooms are made out of concrete. But it makes for a terrible changing surface, even covered in towels. Lucy let me know she hated it, and her screams bounced off the walls and floor like a cloud of frenzied mosquitoes.

It Could Happen to You

We did not swim again for five months. This means I will never know how the tankini looked. Lucy is now too large to wear it. She has also outgrown the first pack of swimming diapers, which cost about eighty cents each. But I'm trying not to think of that. I can always unload them at a garage sale, along with the Baby Einstein video. She's just not getting relativity, either, and I don't know how much more of the music meant for small ears I can stand.

Nor did she enjoy our recent swim. As soon as we got on the pool deck, she went monkey on me, grabbing me with her hands and feet. She clamped down harder once we were in the water. Every part that could grip was doing its best to hang on; I have the cuts to prove it. I tried halfheartedly to float her, but babies do not float when they're in the fetal position. Instead, we just swished around in the water, pretending like it was a giant bathtub. We hugged and chatted. Every once in a while, she smiled, but I think that's because the lifeguard was foxy, and Lucy was topless. Even at seven and a half months, she's well aware of her charms.

The lifeguard just wasn't enough to make for a really fun outing, though. And the whole experience was a reminder of something I've noticed more and more lately: Lucy needs me. It's a different kind of need than the one she had when she was a newborn. Then, I got the feeling that she viewed me as her own personal Dairy Queen franchise. Lucy ate and ate and ate and ate, and for weeks, didn't so much as smile in gratitude. Later, she got liberal with the smiles. Maybe I got a few more than everyone else did, but not many. Pretty much anyone could hold her, and that was fine with Lucy. It was fine with me, too. A friendly baby is something to be proud of.

Lately, though, she's let me know I am her A-Number-One Super Friend. If someone else is holding her and I walk by, she whines, sticks out her arms, and leans toward me. Her eyes bulge, and she makes a noise that sounds like a sewing machine engine in high gear. If she is in her crib, fighting her mortal enemy Mister Sandman, I can't get anywhere within eyeshot. She takes it personally if we look at each other and I don't rescue her.

But I love it. I love making this baby feel happy and secure, even if it means my spine literally goes numb several times a day. The main reason I put up with the freakiness of a tingly back is that I know Lucy won't always feel this way about me. Babies fall in love with their mothers. The point of growing up is claiming independence. And sometimes, this feels like the opposite of love.

I know I created separation from my own mom in all sorts of ways. And this wasn't always easy. Every time we went somewhere together, people would say, "Oh! You look *just* like your mother." No one wants to hear this, especially during the seventies, when your mom is wearing thick, black glasses and plaid pants shaped like trumpet mouths. Even then, I knew those pants were a bad idea, although they were how I used to keep track of Mom in a crowd.

It wasn't that there was anything wrong with how my

mom looked. She was decade appropriate. And even though I'm shorter, I weigh a good fifteen pounds more than she did at my age. She looks way better in pants (still!), and she has the naturally curly hair I deserve but, for some reason, did not get.

The simple fact is that I just wanted to be me. That's the other side effect of growing up as part of the "Free to Be You and Me" generation. You feel it is your right to be you, and when your mother has the gall to look like you, sound like you, and act like you, she's being a real jerk.

If Lucy is anything like me, she'll find lots of ways to assert her independence. And yes, I am aware of the irony there. I'm just hoping she doesn't do anything permanent, like a face tattoo. Or any tattoo, for that matter. This is my future speech to her, which I will no doubt regret because it will be the very sermon that drives her to the tattoo parlor:

Lucy, for crying out loud! Tattoos stretch and fade. That heart may look adorable on your pelvis when you're twenty-one, but when you're thirty-one, with a baby, it's going to have stretched so much it looks like the four parts of a cow's stomach. Have you seen the hole that used to house my navel ring? It's the size of the Grand Canyon!

For now, though, I am loving how she lays her head in the hollow between my neck and shoulders. Its weight is perfect, like the feeling of a softball smacking the heart of your glove.

Come to think of it, I might even have to take her swimming again next week. If I do, I'm hoping that our outing doesn't end up quite like it did last time. The pool is near my parents' house, so we went there afterward for a visit. As I carried Lucy in her car seat, I tripped on the walkway. I am not graceful, and this was a huge wipeout—a belly flop onto concrete that left me flat on the ground, my arms flailing at Lucy's car seat, which had tipped to its side.

My dad saw it happen and raced out to pick her up. She was buckled in, so she was fine, but screaming. I, on the other hand, was thoroughly bashed. Dad held Lucy, while I struggled to stand, looking around for the one person who would make me feel like less of an idiot: my mother.

Uncle

Maybe I hit my head in the fall after our trip to the pool. Or maybe it's just these hideous bruises I still have on my knees. Either way, something unexpected has happened: I have given up.

I wanted to take such perfect care of Lucy. My plans were as follows: I would read, sing, dance, nourish, and clean her. While doing this, I would look neat and trim, keep a perfect house, cook lavish dinners, and advance my writing career without so much as wasting one second on self-doubt or soap operas.

I got as far as the singing part when I realized I was in trouble. I don't know anything but TV theme songs. It was when

I was singing, "Bad boys, bad boys, whatcha gonna do," that I realized something else: I can't dance, either. What's more, I'm not much of a cook, and not even the dog will eat off the floor it's so dirty. Also, I have a bit of a problem with self-doubt.

The worst, though, is that I was trying to do all these things while simultaneously giving Lucy the one thing she really needed. And I'm not talking about rhythm. You can't give what you don't have. Rather, I'm talking about a steady flow of love and attention. The kind you see on TV in baby formula commercials. At first, this wasn't so difficult. When she was a newborn, she slept a lot; I didn't appreciate how much until now. Back then, the challenge was to find the energy to do anything besides loll about and read as I recovered from her birth. Now, Lucy is an eighteen-pound tornado of activity and demands—and I predict, not so boldly, that she's only going to pick up speed from here.

Including her in my every activity requires a lot of muscle. We did vacuum together just this morning, but it's getting ridiculous. It was less of a loving hold than a Heimlich maneuver. The most difficult, though, is when I try to write. Lucy has now taken to leaning forward and typing along with me. It's very cute, but also tends to freeze up the computer. Also, her spelling is atrocious. It's no wonder the phrase is motherhood and apple pie, and not motherhood and novels. The two are tough to combine.

After several exhausting weeks trying to do everything with

Lucy, I realized that I am a failure. Completely and utterly. This realization freed me up to take some sensible advice from Adam, advice he and others have been giving for weeks: Hire a baby-sitter. After giving it a lot of thought, I decided it was better to have some help a few hours a week. During those hours, I'd focus completely on my new career (along with a few housekeeping chores, just to keep things spicy). The rest of the time would be Lucy's. No distractions, as long as you don't count my very bad singing voice, which makes even the cats sit up and look miffed.

It took a little while to find just the right baby-sitter, but we did. She's a twenty-four-year-old Russian named Elena, who loves babies, likes cats and dogs. She also knows how to knit booties. And she has a particularly fetching habit of squeezing Lucy's toes when she arrives for work. This is Elena's third day with Lucy, and so far, everything is going very well. On her first two days, I lurked around them for a good chunk of the time, so that I could answer any questions Elena had. That was my official reason.

My secret reason is that I didn't want Lucy to feel abandoned. When you're a mother, your guilt light goes off the second you start doing something for you, instead of something for your child. Whether you work for the money, or just for the sense of satisfaction, doing anything but tending your child feels like some form of neglect, as if you're pouring acid on the fabric of society.

The truth is, mothers are people, too. And I'm learning that we can do a better job of it if we take care of our own needs, at least for part of the day. And writing is one thing I really, really need to do. That, and stopping the toilet when it's running. It drives me nuts! Still, it's an adjustment having someone else look after Lucy. Although my sisters have taken care of her, it feels different because they're family. Turning her over to a stranger, even if I'm there, is scary at times. I wonder what's going through Lucy's mind, and if she still feels secure and adored.

So, when I do slink upstairs to do some work, I find myself stopping to listen. The first day was the worst. When I heard nothing, I had one thought: Lucy is dead. When I heard her laugh, I thought, *"Drats. Elena is more entertaining than I am."* And when I heard Lucy cry, I thought, "Thank God someone else has to take care of that for once."

Actually, that's not what I thought, though it's making me laugh to say it. A few times when Lucy cried, I went down to feed her. But mostly, I let Elena handle it, because I didn't want Lucy to think all she had to do to summon me during Elena's shift was let out a wail. Elena's quite good at making Lucy feel better. She's also good at finding time to wash clothes while Lucy naps—something I never got the hang of. For the first time in a long time, I'm seeing the bottom of the laundry hamper.

The house, for once, is clean. Lucy is downstairs right now, laughing at her cannibalistic puppet, Duran, who likes to eat baby hands and feet. In forty-five minutes, Elena will go home. I will have gotten some work done, and I'll be ready to think about no one and nothing but Lucy for a while.

I have to say, sometimes giving up is a good thing to do.

The Model Child

You know how, just before you die, your life is supposed to flash before your eyes? I think a similar phenomenon occurs when you do something that you know is really stupid. Instead of the instant replay of your life, you see the hinges fly right off the doors of your mind. Thus unhinged, you feel jiggly and breezy, and thoroughly convinced that the stupid thing you've got planned makes sense.

This is how I felt when I started searching the Internet for child-modeling opportunities for Lucy. I know full well that all mothers think the world would be a better place if highways were lined with their own children's giant, airbrushed faces. But most people have the good sense to realize that this isn't necessarily the best thing for their children, and they don't waste valuable time surfing the Net for contact information. For my lapse in sanity, I blame Lucy. If she weren't so cute, and didn't love to have her picture taken so much, I wouldn't be doing this.

It wasn't always this way. At first, we needed to take a lot of pictures of her, just to get one that didn't make her look like a chapped demon spawn from outer space. Of course, she looked incredibly beautiful to me at the time. Just like a cherub. I blamed the camera for any failure to capture her pulchritude. The camera failed many times. Thousands, in fact.

We've taken at least two thousand pictures of her. According to my calculations, this means we have averaged a picture of her every two and a half hours since she was born. We started when she was only seconds old, and paused only to deal with a broken camera. Out of that mass of pictures, we have about thirty really good ones.

We used to have to take photos in bulk because the sight of the camera was enough to melt any cute expression off Lucy's face. I used to call the smiling Lucy the Yeti, because any time I tried to document her existence, she would disappear and be replaced by a slack-jawed drooler with the occasional case of demonic red-eye. Now, we have to take a lot because she loves the camera and smiles really hard the moment she sees it. It's hard *not* to take a cute picture.

If we have another baby, Adam and I are in big trouble. We made a solemn vow to take equal numbers of pictures of all of our children. He is the fourth of four children, and there is exactly one baby picture of him. He appears in the left corner, dwarfed by both a picnic table and by his adoring sister, who is holding him. At least I think it's him. She might just be holding a nectarine. He's that tiny in the shot.

We do have some early pictures of Lucy smiling, thanks to my dad. His annual Christmas portraits line the wall of the family room, and they are proof of his talent. The first features a smiling baby boy all dressed up in a holiday suit. The second shows a smiling baby girl and happy toddler. The third features two smiling toddlers and a newborn sitting atop a large rock. While it is true that the newborn was dropped seconds after the picture was taken, the point remains that Dad got the money shot before the baby rolled down the hill. The next one features three smiling toddlers and a newborn. Then come four smiling children and yet another newborn. This time, though, the baby was *not* dropped—a sign of progress. And, even when the babies stopped coming, the pictures didn't. We just added baby dolls, cats, and dogs. There's a picture for every year, and we're all smiles in every one. Even the dogs.

Now that I've tried to take pictures of Lucy looking this angelic, I'm amazed my dad did it so well. I'm also amazed that my mom managed to take such good care of all of us, although I remember quite clearly why she didn't want to be in any of the pictures. Any time we were standing still, as we had to for a portrait, she took the opportunity to wash the floor.

I'm also impressed he did it all without losing his head like I have. I am completely certain he didn't even think of contacting modeling agencies on our behalf. And this is not just because my sister once tried to cover a scratch on her face with a piece of Dial soap (see family portrait Number Fourteen). Rather, it's because he knew there were more important things for us to do. Like yard work.

Lately, though, I am over my urge to pursue Lucy's modeling career. Two things cured me: the Web site that featured "baby models" alongside greased-up adult women in thongs, and the bulletin board that reported babies only get $50 for smiling cute for the camera. Like that ex-supermodel Linda Evangelista, Lucy doesn't get out of bed for less than ten thousand a day.

For a smile like hers, I wouldn't settle for a penny less.

The Thing with Lucy's Mouth

In her extremely photogenic little mouth, Lucy has developed a curious new feature. It's a tooth, a front tooth. Only, it's not in the front of her mouth. Rather, it appears to have slid about a half-inch from the center, not unlike where you would expect a vampire's fang to dangle.

We call it the Slider.

And now, the question before us is, "Is the Slider a runaway front tooth, or is Lucy just getting a side tooth first?"

Right now, it's too early to tell. The Slider has only just emerged. This is no surprise, of course. We were expecting a top tooth; we just thought it would appear someplace else. In fact, I was working upstairs one night a couple of weeks ago while Adam was feeding Lucy her dinner. He hollered for me to come right away, because he thought he saw the tooth making its way into the world. I ran down—who wouldn't hurry to see a first look at her baby's top tooth?

As it happened, it was only creamed corn.

The Slider, however, is for real. No vegetable in the world could hurt as much when applied, with pressure, to my bare breast. This pain and suffering is okay, though. A little misery in the name of parenthood is part of the deal. Besides, Adam gets it worse. Every time he carries Lucy in the sling, she kicks him right in the groin, thereby increasing the odds that she will be an only child.

There is another kind of pain, though, that I am handling with less grace. And that is the pain that comes with wondering if this tooth means Lucy has her mouth on sideways. Now I know it would not be the end of the world if Lucy had a few teeth in the wrong places. I've described Adam's unique dental history, and in all fairness, I should also reveal that one of my teeth—a permanent one, no less—came in ten years late, and backward.

But Lucy, up until now, has been so perfect. She has a smile that gives wings to my heart. It's lemon-shaped, huge, and symmetrical. Thinking my silly, worried thoughts, I started surfing the Internet to see if there was any way of telling whether the tooth we're seeing is a front tooth gone amok, or a side tooth that's just coming in a little early. The verdict is unclear. I found a rather vividly named "tooth eruption chart" that labels teeth with a letter between A and E. The "A" and "B" teeth come in first; the "E" teeth, last. The A teeth are in the center of the top and bottom, and the B teeth sit like bookends on either side of them.

It's possible that Lucy's Slider is a B tooth, and is, therefore, perfectly normal. But it's really far to the side, which means she's going to have a helluva gap even if it is normal. She's going to be "lusty and gat-toothed" like the Wife of Bath from the *Canterbury Tales*. We're going to have to sell our kidneys to pay for the braces. We're . . . we're . . .

It's at times like these that I realize I am getting ahead of myself. First of all, the Slider might slide right back into place once it has a little more company. Second of all, it's a baby tooth. She'll be getting a do-over in a few years. Third of all, a snaggletooth smile on Lucy is bound to be as cute as a regular one. Finally, and most important, I love her just the way she is, and however she's going to be.

But that doesn't mean I'm not going to worry. And it's a lot easier to worry about something like a baby tooth than the other things I've feared lately. In fact, I've been so worried, I haven't been able to write about it. I've just wanted the gnawing feeling to go away. It's not, though. Which means it's time for me to start thinking about what I'm going to do if it's actually a problem.

So here goes. All of the child development books I've read mention a couple key things babies should be doing that Lucy is not doing, and hasn't done. One of them seems silly: It's the act of sticking out her tongue, in imitation of Adam and me when we do this. A reputable book said *all* babies could do this, starting at just a few weeks. Lucy has *never* been able to do this—not well, anyway. And she only did it a couple times today, meekly, after Adam spent a few minutes focusing on nothing else. It worries me that Lucy can't really stick out her tongue. Does it mean she doesn't get the fact that she has a tongue, or that we're trying to communicate and she's not getting the clue?

This leads me to my second fear: that Lucy's also not really making the kind of sounds she is supposed to. I was alarmed a couple days ago when I read that four-month-old babies are supposed to be able to imitate sounds their parents are making. Lucy doesn't do this, at eight months. And she was a little over six months old before she made a recognizable "ba" sound—her first, unless you count the "ma" sound she would sometimes make when she was crying really hard.

I mentioned this to the pediatrician at Lucy's six-month checkup. The doctor said she would be worried, but for that detail—that Lucy could say "ma" when she was crying. That wasn't much comfort then, and it's even less now that two months have passed and Lucy is not stringing together multiple syllables, the ba's and ga's that are the hallmarks of healthy baby chatter. It's not that Lucy is silent. She makes noises. Just not the noises that the books say she is supposed to make. When I combine this with my observation that Lucy is also apparently unable to stick out her tongue, it starts to feel ominous.

So, there is my fear, written down at last. That perhaps what we are seeing is just the edge of a problem, just as we are seeing the edge of Lucy's first top tooth. Things are not quite where they should be. I will talk to the doctor about it when we go in for Lucy's nine-month checkup. And I will keep talking to Lucy, every chance I get, so that I feel confident I'm doing everything I can to help her develop speech.

That aside, there's nothing I can do. Lucy is who she is. This may be nothing. All children are different; all human beings are different. The only reason I will ever want her to be like anyone else is just because I know that sometimes, it's our differences that make people reject us. I don't want her to ever feel that kind of pain, although I know it can often be the birthplace of great strength.

Nonetheless, I am feeling it for her and loving her all the more. She is my child. Perfect or not, I would die for her a thousand times, every time feeling grateful for every second I've had her. Except maybe when she bites me with those brand-new teeth. I may be a mother, but I'm still human, after all.

Lucy on the Loose

Since she turned eight months old, Lucy has learned several new tricks. She can crawl on her hands and knees, although she prefers the GI Jane creep, undoubtedly because it matches her short, fuzzy hair better. She can sit herself up and even lurch forward and balance on her knees. Also, she can pull herself up in her crib. And finally, she is a master of the yoga position called the "downward dog."

That's the good news. This is what Lucy has given me. What she has taken away, however, is the last bit of freedom I didn't know I had.

Here's what I mean by that.

It used to be that I could leave Lucy alone for a few moments. Once upon a time, I could pee without filling out an application, paying a fee, and enduring a two-week waiting period. Before Lucy was fully mobile, and before she truly comprehended I was her gravy train with the biscuit wheels, I could leave her for a few moments in her "gym"—an activity mat with two arches full of happy, dangling toys. Lucy would play here for long spans of time, and it really didn't matter to her whether I was right there or not.

Nowadays, I have to plead my case with her when nature calls.

"Lucy," I say, "Mama will be back in thirty seconds. Every once in a while, she really needs to do one of those things you do, only she doesn't have the luxury of wearing a diaper. Believe me, for this half-minute separation, you're going to be fine."

And then I pack her into an object or toy with a five-point safety harness, while she bends her face into a huge frown and turns into a tear factory. The crying is horrible. Not only does Lucy look absolutely pitiful, the running water makes me feel like I have a hog on my bladder.

What's more, Lucy is starting to figure out that these plastic things we call "play yards" and "activity centers" are actually rainbow-colored jails. Whenever I try to put her into either, so I can pick up the living room or eat a sandwich, she looks me up and down. The message is clear: Why should I be in this thing, when there's a) a cat over there who wants to have his tail pulled; b) a remote control I'd like to whap my head with; or c) a magazine that looks positively scrumptious?

Once upon a time, I thought a more independent Lucy would mean a more independent me. Sweet merciful crap, I was an idiot. And I am sure this is just the first of many times I will say that. What I am learning is, the more Lucy grows, and the more independent she becomes, the more she needs me.

It's not the same kind of need she used to have, where she needed pretty much constant holding and feeding. Rather, she needs me to keep her from cracking her head like an egg. The newly mobile Lucy is a menace. She's a danger magnet. If there is a threatening object to be eaten, touched, petted, or head-butted, Lucy crawls for it with all her might. The more dangerous an object is, the faster she crawls. Baby toys never inspire her to action. As I write this, she is at my feet wrapping her neck with the cord of a spare computer keyboard, smiling blissfully.

Baby-proofing is a crock. It doesn't matter if a room has been baby-proofed. That phrase is a myth designed to sell outlet plugs and hearth bumpers. Lucy can turn anything into a dangerous object. The only Lucy-proofed room would be an empty one with padded walls. And then, she would still try to eat the padding.

I'm sure this is why people no longer dress infants in the colonial-era safety garb known as the pudding—a doughnut of fabric tied around the waist. Sure, a pudding probably made for a nice, soft landing. If babies in the old days were anything like Lucy, they got them wet and refused to wear them, and instead, focused their energy on chewing the pudding to ribbons just small enough to pose a choking hazard.

Still, if there were a protective foam suit for infants, I would buy it for Lucy. Only, I'm sure it would be a waste of money because this newly independent baby has also decided she hates wearing clothes and diapers. Getting her dressed and changed has gone from Lucy's favorite part of the day to a wrestling match. Every morning it goes like this: I put Lucy down on her changing pad, which has been taken off the changing table for safety's sake, and she pops back up. I unfold her legs to put the diaper on her; she rolls over and starts making a crawl for the doorway. Up and down, back and forth we go, until both of us are sweaty, crying, and agitated. Lately, I've taken to giving her a big, rubber boot to play with, just to distract her long enough so that her naughty bits are covered. Even with the boot distraction, she's peed on me three times in as many days, because I'm just not fast enough with the diaper.

As Lucy develops the ability to move around, she's also getting much better control with her hands. I have scratches on my arms, chest, and face. It used to be that Lucy would only slash at me with her nails when she was eating. Now, she has the dexterity to pick off the scabs. It's making me realize that both of us would be better off wearing foam suits.

The really crazy thing is, I would have thought that all this extra moving around would make Lucy really tired. The bright side would be that she'd sleep through the night all the time. But a curious side effect is that all her new skills keep her up at night, because she's practicing them. This, at least, is what I read in one of those infant development books.

I'm not sure I believe it. Lucy says nothing about practicing when we try to put her down to sleep at night. The moment after we place her on her back in the crib, she rolls over, stands up, and explains loudly—with *feeling*—that she'd like to be anywhere but there. I try to be firm, but every once in a while, I take her out, and let her fall asleep in my arms. She gets warm and heavy, and I get weepy just looking at her pink cheeks and soft eyelashes.

Independence is a good thing. It's a sign that Lucy is fast turning into a toddler, and I am so proud of all the things she's learning to do. But I confess that I'm secretly glad that in spite of all her accomplishments, she still needs me, all the time.

The truth is, I need her just as much.

The Myth of Mother Knows Best

Whoever said, "Mother Knows Best" is a big, fat liar. Either that, or he was selling something useless door-to-door, like a solar-powered vacuum cleaner. If people actually believed that mothers know best, there is no way there would be so many parenting books out there. I searched an online bookstore and found 34,821 of them—many written by men, and, therefore, people who are not mothers.

Beyond this weighty piece of evidence, however, I have the clincher: If people really believed mothers know best, they would stop giving those of us who currently hold the job title their random bits of unwanted advice. For example: Quite frequently when I take Lucy outside and she's not wearing a hat—and even if she's dressed in two layers of polar fleece and tucked into my coat—old ladies will stop me and chide, "That baby is cold."

What these ladies are not seeing is the speed with which "that baby" is able to yank off her expensive, hand-knit caps. I've actually had to double back a good twelve blocks to pick them up off the sidewalk where she casts them like so much useless litter. Nonetheless, old ladies have stopped to inform me that Lucy is cold at least once a month since last August, when she was born during a heat wave. It has gotten so that I have changed my definition of what makes a woman old. Formerly, all she had to have is what I call "cloud hair"—that frothy, permed confection that says to the world, "I've given up on fashion, hair accessories, and even the comb. I'm sensible: I'm going to steal your parking spot at the grocery store, and onlookers will applaud me for my spunk."

Deluded by this practical haircut, these old ladies—some of them no more than thirty-five—have decided they know a cold baby when they see one. And the cold baby, they have decided, is *that* baby. Meaning the one strapped to your sweaty chest. Why do they say "that baby" and not the gentler "this baby" or the more accurate "your baby"? That I do not know. Maybe it's the chemicals in the perm talking. But there is something communicated by the very word choice, because it is repeated by all the shameless, sleep-glutted people who also say such things as, "That baby should be sleeping through the night by now."

New parents never say this to one another. If you are lucky enough to have a child who has figured out how to sleep like the proverbial baby, instead of like a weasel with hemorrhoids, you may admit your good fortune. But you lower your eyes and summon an air of humility when you do it, so that the gods do not revoke their blessing.

I know. Lucy used to be able to sleep for six hours. Now, we're lucky if she gets two before she stirs, bonks her head while trying to stand in her crib, then starts wailing loud enough to summon help from galaxies far, far away.

For some reason, though, everyone who has gone a good thirty years without the effects of tattered sleep seems to feel perfectly comfortable saying, "That baby should be sleeping through the night right now."

"That baby," I've decided, is a secret code for "you're a dope."

It appears in all sorts of sentences that apply to the way Adam and I are raising Lucy. For example, "How long are you going to nurse 'that baby'?" Or, "I would have thought 'that baby' was a boy, the way you have it dressed."

I know, I know. Stupid questions like these don't even deserve answers. But I can't resist trying to provide them. It's my nature. And it's not as though I'm interrupting my ten-year-old's language arts class for a little nipple time. Lucy's only eight months old. Most recent recommendations suggest nursing a child to her first birthday, if possible. Yes, that may contradict what some of these people heard during the Van Buren administration. The nicest thing I can say to people who think otherwise is "Hey. I'm glad your memory is still working."

As for the feeling that Lucy looks like a boy, well, the truth is that I like red and blue more than I like pink, and I'll also be able to use the clothes again, if I someday have a boy.

I wonder if we mothers bring this on ourselves by buying books and magazines and watching TV shows featuring experts. I know I've bought into a ton of that stuff, and spent a lot of time flipping through magazines to try and figure out how to get Lucy back on the sleep train, among other things. And if that's the case, the irony of it is cruel. We're only trying to do what's best, and we have to suffer through the drive-by parenting of other people, some of whom don't even know the names of our children.

So this is what I'm going to do. I'm going to spend a few days ignoring the books, the magazines, and the guilty bystanders suggesting other ways of raising Lucy than the ones that come naturally. The human species endured an awful long time before parenting books were ever printed. If Lucy and I had been thrust together as a parent-child unit in another era—like the Upper Paleolithic—we wouldn't have had advice manuals, anyway. Just rocks, fur, grubs, and the occasional saber-tooth tiger on a stick. As it is, we're eating better than that and having a pretty great time.

For the next few days, if I feel like letting Lucy sleep in bed next to me, I will. And if she falls asleep better while nursing, so be it. If she goes on another clothing strike like the one she had yesterday, then I'll just let her scoot around in her diaper, hooting and screaming with glee for the better part of an hour. So what if "that baby" ends up being spoiled, as one old lady recently told me was the case? At least I won't have to watch Lucy cry.

So it's resolved. This mother knows best, and is officially going to ignore all the advice from strangers and experts 'round the world. I'm going to ignore it for at least three days.

Because that's how long it's going to take the bookstore to deliver me my copy of *Secrets of the Baby Whisperer.* Deep down, I want that baby to get a good night's sleep again. We sure could use it.

Chapter 9

Getting a Life

✴

To achieve the impossible dream, try going to sleep.
                                                    —Joan Klempner

Also, try going out for dinner and not talking about the baby.

The Leather Anniversary

Before Adam and I had Lucy, we were often at each other's side for at least twenty hours a day. There were certain activities we *never* shared, though. Adam never pumiced my heels or tweezed my eyebrows. I never offered to spray his feet with fungicide. Also, Adam put his pants on; I put my pants on—never each other's. Not on purpose, anyway. Until I got pregnant, this was a foundation for a happy marriage.

And then, toward the fat and bitter end, the last wall crumbled and Adam began tying my shoes. I couldn't see my feet, let alone bend and commune with them. Because my one pair of slip-ons was starting to stink with the summer heat, I just gave up. Somehow, though, our marriage survived. And as they say, turnabout is fair play. Just last week, Adam had to ask me to help him put on his belt. The reason? Lucy. He was holding her, and she is now so big, it takes two hands to keep her from launching herself onto the ground. Whatever the reason, though, I was happy to return the favor and help get Adam dressed. I'll take dignity wherever I can find it. You have to, when you go out in public with Cheerios stuck to your rear end.

Later that night, Adam came home and said he had learned something about himself. Curious, I asked for detail. Adam is far more likely to talk about comic books than personal growth. It was the belt, he said. He'd threaded it through his loops the same direction all his life. And I had done it the opposite way, giving him trouble every time he had to unbuckle it.

A more insecure person might wonder what her husband was doing unbuckling his belt all day long. Was it all the free soda at work? Or was it something else? Someone else? Thanks to all the free Fresca he has access to, I don't need to wonder these things about Adam.

Instead, what I started thinking about is the habits that we have—things we don't even notice until something changes and we can't do the things the way we've always done them, no matter how comfortable it is. Before Adam and I had Lucy, we were so comfortable with each other and our routines.

Our condo was pretty messy, but it didn't matter because we were never there. Also, we had a maid come every other week to prevent serious funk build-up—this was our first anniversary gift to each other.

Adam and I never fought. I can't even remember disagreeing about anything, except about olives. Adam is a baby on that count, and chicken cacciatore is not as good without them, no matter what he says. I used to marvel, sometimes, at how easy marriage was. Mom was crazy to have told me otherwise all these years. Or so I thought.

Lucy has changed everything. Forget about the messed-up belt loop. Having a child has been like wearing shoes on our hands. Everything is that much harder to do. And I finally am starting to understand why, for most people, marriage requires more effort than deciding whether to have pizza or lasagna for dinner. Often, so many things change you have to rebuild the foundation your relationship stands on.

Adam and I have gone out on two dates without Lucy since she was born nine months ago. During our first date, we looked at each other over our plates of chicken and fish and blinked. Here is how our conversation went:

"Wonder how Lucy is doing?"

"Probably fine."

"But maybe she's not."

"Okay, let's go home."

On our second date, we did a little bit better.

"Lucy wouldn't like these chairs."

"No."

"The salad is too spicy for her."

"Oh yeah, too spicy."

"Think she's sleeping?"

"Let's go find out."

Last Saturday night, Lucy was in bed by eight o'clock, and we had a rare opportunity to have a conversation, maybe share a glass of wine or watch a romantic movie. Instead, we watched the video of Lucy's first six months.

"She was so tiny."

"Yes. Tiny."

"And her legs."

"Yes, tiny."

And it's not just that all of our conversations revolve around Lucy. Other things have changed, as well. At my last checkup, my doctor asked about birth control. "I'm using the barrier method," I said. "Lucy sleeps between us."

It's pathetic. Yesterday was our third anniversary. It's the "leather anniversary," I learned while pondering gift ideas. This is a cruel tradition. Leather is the stuff that sexy pants and whips are made of. When you have a new baby, leather is one of those things that go on the "see you in ten years list." It's right out. You're too fat for the pants and too tired for the whip. The third year of marriage, at least for people with small children, should be celebrated with rubber, preferably the chewy kind that binkies are made out of. This is something people like us have some use for.

Getting a Life

We did get fairly close to a wild-and-crazy leather experience during our anniversary dinner. We parked in front of a sex hall in Seattle's Pike Place Market district. It wasn't the Lusty Lady, the famous sleaze establishment with very clever and naughty puns. "We'd like to spank the Academy" appeared at Oscar time. Rather, the place we parked was quite a bit more downscale, with window displays that would have left Lucy hungry.

These days, though, I'll take it. True romance isn't about leather, sweat, or even the hilarity of suggestive puns. It's something you know you've got when you can look at your baby chasing down a Cheerio on the carpet, and she looks so much like her dad, you can't help but think about him, even when he's busy running an important business meeting like the ones you no longer attend. True romance is having someone to help you through the 1:30 A.M. tearfests. It's having someone let you sleep in while he plays with the baby. It's having a friendship that stays strong and exciting and funny, even when everything changes around it.

If someone had told me three years ago what my life would be like today, I might have run away rather than face the mess and chaos. But this is why we can't see the future, because most of us aren't wise enough to know how much joy comes with the struggle. It's during these challenging times that I find myself with one thought eclipsing all the rest: I am so glad I have someone to share this with, and so glad that person is Adam.

It Could Happen to You
How to Put a Baby to Sleep

Parenting books say babies are capable of sleeping through the night starting at three months. "Capable of" does not mean the same thing as "willing to." For example, Lucy was doing a good job of sleeping through the night until we moved into our house and she decided our bedroom was warmer and more comfortable than hers. She went from sleeping for eight hours to sleeping for two, no matter what we tried. In my experience, if your baby is younger than one and already sleeps through the night, feel lucky. If not, then continue to follow these simple steps for a few more months. You'll get there. At least that's what people have told me.

The twenty-one easy steps

Putting a baby to sleep is a very simple task, though for some reason, it befuddles new parents everywhere.

Adam and I have managed to get Lucy to sleep for as long as twenty minutes straight using this simple, nonpatented formula. It's revolutionary, really. If I had the time, I'd write a book about it, just so I could knock that irritating Baby Whisperer and all of her gratuitous uses of the word cadswallop right off the best-seller list.

But I don't have enough time. Most of my waking minutes are spent putting Lucy to sleep using this method, which as I have said is not only very simple but also is poolfroof. I mean foolproof.

Getting a Life

Step 1: Make sure it's time to get baby ready for bed. You may be disoriented, but you do not want to skip this step. Clocks are reliable tools for this, though in a pinch, you can rely on that round, hot yellow thing in the sky. If the yellow thing is near where the sky and the earth make a line (can *anyone* remember what that's called?), then it's probably just about time to get baby ready for bed.

Once you have looked at the clock and confirmed that yes, it is six-fifteen *in the morning,* then it's time to begin. The baby has already been up for an hour, anyway, playing pat-a-cake on your husband's cheeks. And if she doesn't get her rest, where will she find the energy to repeat this glorious process tomorrow?

Step 2: Feed the baby breakfast. It is a fact universally acknowledged that babies cannot go to sleep at night without a good breakfast, preferably one smeared in their hair and tucked into their folds. Another essential part of a balanced breakfast is to spread chunky remnants of it all over the high chair. This gives you the opportunity to use that crème brûlée blowtorch that in all likelihood will never see a dinner party.

Step 3: Have a nice cup of decaffeinated coffee. There's nothing quite like it to blast you through the morning. While you are sitting on the floor drinking anticoffee, the baby can play beside you. No matter how many toys she has and how widely she has spread them, your cup of hot coffee will be the most interesting thing in the room, followed by the irritable (and sleeping) cat.

Step 4: Wash the baby. You would no sooner put a crusty child to bed than you would get in your own bed wearing the shoes you used to mow the lawn. That would mean you would then have sheets to wash. Everyone knows that laundry breeds fine all by itself in the hamper; it's senseless for you to add to the orgy.

It's best to wash the baby in the bathtub. Showers are not recommended for this, as babies do not yet know how good a shower feels in the morning. Sadly, you do, and you rarely get to take one uninterrupted. But this is because you are rushing through Step 5. See below.

Step 5: Put baby down for her morning nap. You notice she is rubbing her eyes. Ideally, you have finished with Step 4 (baby washing) before this happens, or you will find yourself wondering how to get oatmeal out of eyelashes.

Step 6: Apologize to the baby for trying to put her in a bed made out of nails. Yes, you can't see the nails. But she can feel them, insinuating their pointy tips into the soft, perfect flesh of her back. She lets you know about the nails by screaming, rolling over, and bonking her head on the crib.

Step 7: After verifying that the nails on the crib mattress have left the building, put baby down for her morning nap again.

Step 8: Apologize again.

Step 9: Repeat until baby is worn out.

Step 10: Begin your shower.

Step 11: Just as you've soaped your hide, you hear the sound of baby bonking her head and screaming. What to do? What to do? Hurry and finish shower. Wrap yourself in a towel. Pick up baby, while the towel unwraps itself, showing the world your pale and flabby rear end.

Step 12: Put on clothes with one hand, while entertaining the baby with another. Remember, a happy baby is a baby who goes to sleep easily.

Step 13: It's lunchtime for baby. Repeat Steps 4 and 5.

Step 14: Make your own lunch with one hand, while holding baby in the other. Explain to her that you would like to give her a bite of your sandwich, but she only has three teeth. Be firm. You already turned the dog into an incorrigible beggar, and it would be even more embarrassing to do this to your child.

Step 15: It's playtime again. Playtime is necessary because it tires a baby out, leaving her a prime candidate for nighttime sleeping. Options include: going for a walk; eating fur and bread crumbs off the floor; and trying to trick her into thinking laundry is fun.

Step 16: Time for an afternoon nap. You read somewhere that nine-month-old babies take three hours' worth of naps each day. This means yours is due to sleep for two hours and 40 minutes because she only slept for 20 minutes in the morning.

Step 17: After verifying repeatedly that the crib mattress does not, in fact, have scorpions scuttling about all over it, put the baby down for her afternoon nap. As you walk away from the nursery, think about all the things you can accomplish in this grand two hours and 40 minutes that you have coming. Is there dirty laundry? Great! You will get it clean. Dishes in the sink? Now's your chance to wash them. Were you hoping to finish that book proposal your agent has been hounding you for? Do it!

Step 18: Hear the baby wake up, just as you hit the bottom of the stairs.

Step 19: It's playtime again. Although you may feel as though you cannot lift your head off the carpet, the truth is that you are really discovering how educational it is for your child to use your body as a jungle gym. Admire her strength and dexterity as she crawls over you, drooling and laughing.

Step 20: Dinnertime. Yours, hers, your husband's? The cats and dog? It doesn't matter. Everyone's hungry. Brown pellets all around, unless your husband is cooking, in which case dinner will be very tasty.

Step 21: Bedtime is finally here. That moment you've been working toward all day, so you need to prop your eyelids open so that you can enjoy it. Once your eyelids are open, simply hand the baby over to her daddy. He will take her upstairs, change her diaper, put on her jammies, and then perform what he calls "the ritual."

Some thirty minutes later, he will walk down the stairs, triumphant. The house will be quiet. You might even hear the rosebushes scratching against the walls, stirred gently to life by a cool evening breeze. All is well in the world. The baby is sleeping. You and your husband can have a nice talk about how you spent your day. That's because it'll be at least two hours before baby wakes up again.

And then, you can start all over.

The Age of the Cheerio

This is the dawning of the age of the Cheerio. I had no idea what that would mean, until Lucy was capable of eating them. But as I am learning, it means everything.

Lucy's Cheerio-readiness means she has finally progressed past the stage of early infancy known as "mitten hand." Babies with mitten hand can't pick up tiny objects because they use their fingers as one, clumsy counterpoint to their wee thumbs. As developmental limitations go, this is not a bad one. Babies with mitten hand cannot grab your nipple and twist it slowly, as you might when you're trying to pick up radio signals from distant galaxies.

But all parents, even ones with sore nipples, want to see their children gain full use of their fingers. How would Lucy ever learn to run the washing machine otherwise?

Once I was confident in Lucy's pincer grip, as the next stage is called, I started giving her Cheerios, just two or three, to tide her over while I prepared her breakfast. She put one in her mouth right away. Not because she knew it was food, but because she puts everything into her mouth: briefcase straps, shoelaces, zipper tabs, cat fur, dog fur, sunglasses, remote controls, CDs, magazines. It's her way of saying hello, I guess.

This time, though, she liked the taste of what was in there. She crunched. She swallowed. She went back for more. And so began a new ritual of giving Lucy a heap of Cheerios before every meal. While it's true that her diet now consists of more oat fiber than such a small body can handle gracefully, at least I know she's not eating the equivalent of a heart attack on a high chair tray.

Lucy is as happy as could be when she has her mouth full of Cheerios. While I do the microwave dance to pass the eighteen seconds her mushy food requires for warming, she laughs and shows me how well her four teeth work. And because I have been at this parenting thing for just over nine months now, I have learned to take something that makes the baby happy and abuse it for as long as its power lasts. I used to do this with the Gymini, then the Baby van Gogh video. When all else failed, those tools would pump Lucy full of cheer. These days, it's Cheerios. When she starts getting fussy in the late morning, boom! Out comes a handful. When she can't be consoled in the afternoon, but won't go down for a nap, Cheerios roll to the rescue.

The only time Cheerios have failed me is on the way home from the warehouse grocery store, where we bought a giant box of them. Lucy cried for ten miles, which is a very difficult thing to take when your husband is taking all the red lights we were getting as personal insults. I dumped a huge handful of Cheerios in Lucy's car seat, hoping they'd work their crunchy magic. But they didn't, and we had to stop at a coffee shop and give Lucy a little floor time so she could come down from the overstimulation that happens to all of us, baby or not, when we warehouse-shop.

In just three weeks, we have gone through that coffin-sized box of Cheerios, a box so large we have to keep it in the basement. Of course, only a small portion of these has been eaten. By Lucy, anyway. The dog has had a ton. She always has Cheerio breath lately, but this is an improvement. And it's the first time in nine months that the dog had a reason to be glad Lucy's here. Now she sleeps in the baby's room, instead of ours.

Another 42,000 or so Cheerios have perished underfoot. It's a sickening sound, not unlike that of a bug being crushed. And it means I have to sweep the kitchen several times a day. It's either that or make like I'm decorating with a beach theme, because a graveyard of trampled Cheerios looks an awful lot like sand. The bright side is that it would finally give me a use for the very unattractive tropical-colored beach bag that's sitting in the basement next to the Cheerios box.

The rest of the uneaten rings have all become part of the grand biology experiment known as the Cheerio life cycle. When they are born, Cheerios are puffy and pale—the lovely color of coffee that's been heavily laced with milk. A Cheerio that has been loosed from the box may die young and beautiful, whether eaten or trampled. Or, it may die a slower death, trapped in Lucy's clothing or worse—her diaper. These Cheerios tumble out far from the kitchen, and at the most unexpected times. Once, a whole handful poured out of Lucy's onesie when Adam was changing her.

Though the dog might find one of these stray Cheerios and

put it out of its misery, more often they just pick up hair and start to shrink. Compare a fresh Cheerio to one of the more worldly ones and you start to wonder what is it about Cheerios that makes them shrink as soon as they hit the free world? Are they cursed?

The worst Cheerio death happens to the ones that have been in Lucy's mouth or wet hands. They shrink, pucker, and eventually turn mahogany-dark. They're the shrunken heads of the cereal world, grim reminders of the fact that a Cheerio's life is not as cheery as the name implies. But what would you expect from a cereal that once gave out fake Confederate money and toy guided missiles as toy surprises?

Now that I think about it, I realize that the Cheerio experience, with all the grimness that it brings to mind, is a little like becoming a parent. You start out round, plump, and beautiful—full of nutrition and cheer. And then, over time, you get dark and shriveled. Definitely worse for the wear. You may find yourself chewed, sprawled on the carpet, stuck to the kitchen floor, or a lot closer to the inside of a baby's diaper than you ever expected to be.

But somehow, you know this is your destiny.

It's too bad no one packs a guided missile inside of you as a toy surprise. There's a beach bag by the Cheerios box in the basement that I would kind of like to blow up.

It Could Happen to You

Pets vs. Babies

What's the difference between pets and children?

If you had asked me before I had Lucy, I would have said, "Easy. One kind sheds fur; the other kind dirties diapers." Adam and I are the sort of people who treat our pets as if they are children. We traded a nearly new queen-sized bed for a king early in our marriage, just so we could accommodate the dog and the cats with us at night.

We continue to do this, even though Adam is horribly allergic to both cats and dogs. The sexy as hell nighttime ritual goes something like this: Take anti-coughing pill. Huff on flying-saucer-shaped inhaler. Spray allergy medicine up nose, twice. Kiss good night. Sink into cloud of fur.

We love the animals. They're part of the family, even if one cat is a surly bastard, the other cat is dumb as plankton, and the dog has a heavy-breathing problem that would get us arrested if she knew how to use a phone. None has the slightest respect for a sleeping baby. They've wakened Lucy more times than we can count, to the point where we've wondered, Is this their revenge against us, for bringing the small, hairless beast into the family?

Their faults aside, home wouldn't be home without them. There's something about the clicking of dog toenails following you about and the thwirr of a cat on your lap to remind you that your life is full. As full as your vacuum cleaner bag—and then some.

Before Lucy crawled her way into the world, I thought I knew how much you could love an adorable creature that depended on you for its survival. I took the dog with me everywhere I possibly could, and to a few places I probably shouldn't. (Once, a newsroom colleague used an anonymous message board to accuse Misty of infesting the place with fleas. As if!)

When Misty had a tumor in her chest, and I had one in mine, hers came out first. Every time I had to tie her up somewhere—outside the grocery store, for example—I could feel my heart banging in my chest. What if someone stole her? What if some world-hating teen taunted her cruelly with a stick of jerky? What if? What if? I was not completely insane in my fears. Misty is a superlative beast, more human than canine. She has a beautiful white face and Cleopatra eyes, and she can't help but grin at everyone she sees.

When Misty, Lucy, and I are out for a walk, passersby are as likely to say "Beautiful dog!" as they are to say "Beautiful baby!" (Why is it that no one ever says, "Wow, you're one hot mama!"?)

I had Misty for eight years before Lucy came along. So it was fascinating to realize that as much as I love her, I love Lucy even more. It's like Misty's love for dog kibbles vs. her love for baked goods. Dog kibbles are great to have around every day. But the baked goods . . . they're enough to make a girl do crazy things.

And the truly strange part was that I felt this way, even early on, when Misty and the cats both showed a lot more affection than Lucy did. While Lucy lay on her back, blinking, the cats would both rub their faces on my shins. And while Lucy demanded special favors from my breasts, Misty would bring me gifts. Sometimes unwanted gifts, such as dirty diapers. But it's the thought that counts.

Lucy's rapid-fire development for the first nine months of her life helped her catch up somewhat to the pets. No, she didn't amuse us by contorting into funny positions and licking herself. Nor did she fetch, purr, or warn us loudly about the vicious deliveryman at the front door. She could sit, roll over, and gnaw as well as any of the animals, though. And she showed significantly more excitement than the cats at our presence.

Even though she was the favorite pet, she was still a pet. Once she realized how great solid food is, she even started begging like one.

Recently though—just a few days shy of her ten-month birthday—Lucy has demonstrated that she is rapidly leaving the cats and dog in the dust. Her days of being the fourth pet are over. My evidence of this, not surprisingly, relates to food. While the cats and dog have never once let us forget a meal, while they hound us constantly for bites—beaming their sorrowful eyes straight in our direction—Lucy has started doing something quite curious. She has started sharing her food.

She takes great delight in taking handfuls of whatever she's eating—bread, cereal, beans—and thrusting them upward.

"Here," the gesture says. "Eat this." Could this be altruism? Love for us? The desire to take what is hers and make it ours? Is she, I wonder, giving something back?

The pets have never done anything like this. If Adam and I died, they'd gnaw the flesh right off our bones, and then complain that we tasted stringy. (Except Misty. She would look doleful, and then thump her tail in solemn thanks afterward. But mostly because we finally didn't stop her from eating bones.)

Lucy's gesture, I learned, after taking a bite of the very soggy hunk of pita she had thrust in my direction, had nothing to do with altruism. As soon as I ate it, she laughed and laughed, not unlike a cartoon hyena. And that, I realized, was the really big difference between pets and kids. Your pets might eat your very flesh when you're dead. But your kids do something much, much worse.

They recognize you for the hapless fool you are, so much in love that you'd eat their already chewed-on food.

And then they laugh at you.

Lucy's First Word

I have discovered another myth of parenthood. At least I think I have. And that is the myth of baby's first word. According to the myth, baby's first word is pronounced clearly and loudly. It is often accompanied by the music of harps floating down from a sky lightly padded with clouds. And it sounds like this: Mama.

What I have learned is that baby's first word doesn't really go like this at all. Rather, it sounds more like this: Bickie.

Allow me to explain. Our new nanny, Laramie, came back all breathless from a trip to the park. "I may be crazy," she said. "But I think Lucy is trying to say bird. She keeps pointing at birds and saying boowee."

"Yeah, yeah," I thought. *"You're not crazy, Laramie. Just insane. There's no way Lucy could be saying bird right now. She's not even ten months old. She hasn't babbled the way she is supposed to. And I've been paying her to practice saying Mama, all to ensure that on the glorious day when she says it, my position as the center of her universe is sealed."*

What I said was, "Hmmm. Even if she is making that sound, it's unlikely that she's connecting it with an actual bird."

Nonetheless, Lucy and I started spending a lot more time studying the bird's nest outside the kitchen window—the one that has bewitched her, at the expense of my efficient baby-feeding program—for several months. I finally had to turn the high chair the other way a while back so Lucy would stop looking at the damn birds, and start respecting the spoon.

Then, a few days after the boowee incident, something interesting happened. Lucy, Adam, and I took a little vacation. We rented a cabin yards from the beach, in a protected inlet that twinkled like hammered silver underneath the setting sun. One evening, as we barbecued a couple of steaks and some corn, a seagull the size of a terrier landed on the deck rail right next to the grill.

Lucy pointed to it and said, "B-b-b-b-irdddhhhuh." This touched off a major debate between Adam and me.

Did she say "bird"? Or was it, as he claimed, "bickie"?

The one thing we did not debate was the fact that Lucy had pointed to the giant seagull, and she had uttered a word very close to the one we English-speaking adults apply to winged, egg-laying creatures with feathers. As unlikely as it was, Lucy had said her first word. And the word . . . was bird. More or less, anyway.

My brother-in-law Michael clued me in to the fact that unlike what I was expecting as payoff for all those hours where Lucy and I rehearsed the fine art of saying "mama," a baby's first word pretty much happens when parents decide it has happened. Lucy was pointing at a bird, saying something that sounded an awful lot like bird. As far as Adam and I were concerned, it was time to get out the camcorder and send her application tape to Stanford. Birdbrain nothing! This baby is clearly a genius.

After that, Adam and I became overbearing parents and presented Lucy with far too many opportunities to say bird. I think she got bored with it. Either that, or self-conscious, because half the time, her eyes would get wide and she would press her lips into the line necessary for producing the "B" sound . . . and then she would exhale quietly, tentatively. Buhhhhh.

The message was fairly clear: *"Quit pressuring me. Wait till next week, when I'm ten months old."* Only she doesn't have the words to say this. She had to use the word she had and modify her delivery. Clever baby. And no, I am not reading too much into the situation. If that were the case, I would also claim that Lucy can now say "kitty," even though the most that has come out of her mouth in the vicinity of the cat is a sloppy khehhh.

I might also claim that she can say "bye" because she once waved and said a tiny "bye" to Laramie a minute or so after Laramie left the house. I'm not saying that she can say bye. All I'm saying is she *might* be able to say it. Put two of those "byes" with her other word, bird, and she's got a good start on a Broadway career. But perhaps, Lucy doesn't need Broadway because she has added a new word to her repertoire, a word that could lead her to a career in broadcast journalism: hi.

And this time around, I am certain she means it. When she sees the dog, she says, "hi." When I'm lounging on the sofa, having a moment of denial that my day largely consists of crawling very fast after Lucy, she pulls herself up, breaks into a huge smile and says . . . "hi." She's even taken to greeting the small baby who sometimes grins at her from the mirror.

She is not saying Mama. When I even practice the Mama sound with her, she fakes me out by making the "m" shape with her lips, then curling it upward into a silent Mona Lisa smile.

As with the Mona Lisa, the reason for that smile is a mystery. I think I've decoded it, though. Lucy knows more than she lets on—and she's a master at toying with my heart.

Lucy Learns a Lesson

The most incredible thing has started to happen. Lucy's brain is blooming. She is starting to understand words—and not just single words, like dog, biscuit, daddy, and bird. She understands entire sentences. While sitting down next to Lucy, I said, "Where is your ball?"

Lucy left her spot in front of my knees and swiveled her head until she spied the squishy little soccer ball she's been playing with lately. She crawled to it as fast as she could, then dribbled it back to me.

I just about dropped my cup of coffee. Lucy plays fetch!

Perhaps this shouldn't have flipped my wig. Fetch is a logical progression for a creature who can sit up, beg, and roll over, which she does religiously when I am trying to change her diaper. If only I could paper train her, she would make a very fine little dog.

But she isn't a dog, of course. With dogs, you can guarantee obedience and fidelity—even happiness—with a pocket full of brown pellets. Although Lucy would dearly love to eat pet food from the bowl, I don't think a taste for it is going to get her into college. In all likelihood, she'll outgrow her taste for kibble by the time calculus comes along.

So, how can I be a good parent, if I haven't even been able to train the dog to stay off the couch? I don't know. But I'm doing my best, and there are some results.

For example, Adam and I have taught Lucy how to find our noses. When I ask, "Lucy, where is Mama's nose?" she points to the correct bulge of flesh and cartilage almost 100 percent of the time. She sometimes sticks her finger up it, so I have to take off points. And she has not yet managed to locate her own nose, which means I still have to remove her boogers for her. Still more points off the total. But this is a fine accomplishment for a child who is not yet eleven months old. She has an entire lifetime to learn how to pick her own nose.

She is also learning to recognize that quintessential barnyard animal, the pig. Using her stuffed pig as a reference, she can point to the pig on the page of her *Barnyard Dance* book most of the time. This piece of knowledge will be essential if she is ever to appreciate *Charlotte's Web, Babe,* or any breakfast meat. Later, a love for both the living pig and its pan-fried meat will help her understand the concept of hypocrisy. And when she understands that, she won't protest when I tell her that breakfast is the most important meal of the day, while I skip it for a skull-sized mug of coffee and one of last night's brownies.

But I would be wise to focus first on simpler concepts. For

starters, the concept of "That Hurts Mama." This applies largely to my nipples. Biting and twisting hurt. So does using the nipple to pull oneself up into the standing position. Lucy does not yet grasp this concept. If she did, she would stop grasping me where it hurts. I hope. Perhaps she's trying to teach me something about the irony. If this turns out to be the case, I will have much to write about later on, when her vocabulary is larger.

I would also like her to understand the difference between laundry that has been folded, and laundry that is okay to wave like a flag. For some reason, Lucy finds stacked and folded laundry the most compelling, and she spends a little time every day unloading the napkins and placemats from their little cupboard.

Her technique has improved steadily. She is now agile enough to unfold things faster than I can get them folded, which leaves her plenty of time to crawl into the kitchen to eat cat food while I am refolding. Ultimately, though, the unfolding enterprise is counterproductive. If she spent less time unfolding in the first place, she would have more time to plan a successful cat food caper. The usual outcome, unhappily for Lucy, is that I swoop her up just before she sinks her mitts into the bowl. Time management, Lucy. I suggest you learn it.

Adam wants her to learn another lesson in the food category. He calls it, "That's Lucy's Food." When Lucy eats bananas, for example, she likes to give some to me, some to Adam, some to Misty, a little gobbet to the cats and a meaningful offering for the Floor Gods. She also likes to spackle the cracks in her high chair with it. This is very generous of Lucy, but it also means she hasn't eaten, and the room and all its inhabitants need cleaning.

But this lesson is probably less important than "That is dangerous!" I can tell this phrase only confuses her lately. Every time I say it, she continues to play with the lamp cord underneath the desk. Would it really be safer for me to work by candlelight? The world is a strange place when that is true.

Perhaps she's not confused, though. I'm starting to suspect she's ignoring me. I have these little curtains in my office, with long cords that are a known strangling hazard. Lucy loves playing with them. Every time I say, "Lucy, that is *dangerous*," she turns and twinkles her eyes at me, with the throat-sized curtain pull in her mouth. She actually uses it as a teething toy, which is why "remove curtains from office" is on my list of things to do.

While we're on things Lucy should learn, but won't, I will add: "Don't You Think It's About Time for Bed?" I am really getting into fantasy territory here, I know. We can no longer get her anywhere near her crib without starting off a shriek-fest. I have to bite my fist when I think back to the time I could lay her gently in the crib, and she would turn her head, close her eyes, and float off to sleep. Little did I know then that Lucy would later fall in love with the world and would fight hard to stay conscious every minute of the day.

She is showing some signs of improvement in this area,

thankfully. This morning, just before three o'clock, I was tucking her back under her blanket after a little drink of milk. As is my habit, I stroked her back, waiting for her breathing to grow slow and regular. It wasn't happening. Lucy kept jerking her arm up, fiddling with the covers.

"What's she doing?" I thought. And then it hit me. Lucy was trying to tuck in her teddy bear. I slid the blanket over both of them, and Lucy turned to the bear and said, "Hi," with the sweetest little voice in the world. Then she fell right asleep.

It was the most loving thing I've seen her do, and it hit me right then and there that Lucy already knows the only lesson that matters. Walking back into my room, with a lump in my throat, I thought, *"Where did you ever learn that?"*

As it turns out, putting Teddy to bed is something she learned from Adam. Why am I not surprised?

Was I Ready for This?

Lucy is almost a year old. It's a little late, but I'm starting to wonder if I was really ready to be a mother. I thought I was, of course. I had everything I thought I needed: a happy marriage, solid finances, and a sincere desire to dress someone tiny in cute things. Someone besides Adam's cat. In the last year, I've learned these things are not enough. What you also need, if you're going to be a parent, is tough skin. And I'm not speaking metaphorically here. Not entirely, anyway.

It Could Happen to You

I've spent several months of Lucy's first year covered in scabs that Lucy has given me with her fingernails while nursing intently, trying to avoid going into the crib, or maybe just checking me for fleas. She does the same things to the pets, although I do not have their coat of protective fur, except on my legs, which I no longer have time to shave regularly. Why can't Lucy just scratch those? I don't know. It's not as if she doesn't try. Or perhaps the long leg hair is working its magic. Either way, Lucy hangs on my pant leg almost constantly as she perfects the art of walking. Why, she's even pulled my pajama bottoms right off.

Which brings me to another thing you need to be a parent: pants that stay up. When you're nursing, you have to get used to flashing yourself in public regularly. Not everyone appreciates it, but most enlightened people are willing to support a baby's right to eat, even if that includes a little unbidden boob now and then. I don't know of anyone, however, who feels the same way about pants coming down. This is the sort of thing people call the police over. And even if that doesn't happen, it's a little humiliating, because you're still wearing the same stretched-out underpants you wore when you were pregnant and refused to buy the giant kind.

Which brings me to the next thing I've learned one needs to be a parent: a total loss of pride. Many, many times, you'll find yourself within earshot of other adults saying things like, "Yes. See the birdie. Birdie flies and lands on tree. Tree is green and full of birds. Birds!" It wouldn't be so bad if babies held up their part of the discussion. But they don't. You end up sounding like one of those people whose idea of conversation is, "Enough about me, though. What do *you* think of me?"

There's a variation on the pride theme. And that is acceptance—acceptance that other people will frequently think you're having delusions of prodigy. When your baby learns tricks, such as clapping, saying "hi," and pointing to the pig in her favorite book, she will *never* do this in front of an audience. Everyone will think you're just imagining she really can do these things. Which in some cases is probably true. After all, everyone who's ever had a baby knows what it's like to have the world's most beautiful and talented child.

And if you're going to celebrate your child's genius, it seems only right that you accept her flaws, or at least come up with a plan for accommodating them. It took me thirty years to achieve perfection myself. I am giving Lucy, who is brilliant, ten years to do the same. I don't know what I'll do then if she isn't perfect. I'm pretty attached to her, and don't imagine I'll try to sell her on eBay or anything. But I will keep my options open.

This brings to mind another quality parents really ought to have: flexibility. You can be a very, very organized person coming into the parenthood game. You can be so good at getting things that people regularly compliment you on this trait. If you have a job outside the house, it's the sort of thing that gets you nice, fat raises. You might even get addicted to that "I'm done!" sensation.

You have to get over this. With a baby, and I'm just betting, with a child, nothing is ever really done. It's just momentarily stable. If you're lucky. Changed the diaper? Guess what. She just pooped. Washed her toys? Guess what. The dog is slobbering on Buzzy Bee. Dishes done? Not any more. Baby just had a sippy cup of milk. And then she threw it on the floor you just cleaned, and the lid came off and the cat walked through it and now there are milky paw prints between the kitchen and the family room. Also, the baby wants carpet time, which means you need to be there to make sure she doesn't bonk her head, bite the lamp cord, or make the cat do something everyone will later regret. I'm not saying there are no fringe benefits of parenting. It's just that you can't get into this game expecting your life will go from good to perfect. If anything, it'll go from good to seriously messed up.

If you're like the silent, skulking majority, you won't have had a good night's sleep since before the baby was born. Of course, you do hear about those infants who start sleeping through the night at six weeks. And although they're probably just such dullards they wouldn't be interested in the world around them if it was shaped like a giant, leaking nipple, it doesn't make you feel all that much better that you're raising a genius, because the 2 A.M. screaming has left you with seriously diminished hearing. In fact, you might not even be able to enjoy her playing violin concertos in two years if this continues.

When you start thinking like that, though, you just have to feel glad you mastered the concept of "one day at a time" before you became a parent. You can't worry about today's hearing loss ruining tomorrow's recital. More generally, if you're stuck in the middle of a difficult day—let's say, a teething day, or the kind of day that happens after baby has eaten a lot of corn—you can't give in to your fear that all is lost and you will never shower before noon again. Rather, it's just this day you're living that is tough. Tomorrow is sure to be easier, for tonight, almost certainly, your baby will sleep straight through.

Mastering the art of taking things one day at a time is easiest when you've also cultured with a healthy ability for denial. Is minivan ownership starting to look attractive to you? No! You're just developing more appreciation for old people— people with kids in elementary school. Is that poop on your arm? Nope! You're just going to scrub that wet lint with antibacterial soap for kicks, that's all.

And speaking of kicks, it's probably a good idea to define going to Costco as a date with your husband before you have a child, so it won't feel that lame when a trip to Costco actually is a date. Adam and I had a great one yesterday. It even cost the same as a really, really nice dinner out with a group of friends. We spent $30 on diapers, which is about what a fancy bottle of wine costs. A bottle of wine, or a month's supply of diapers—I say, the diapers are a lot more fun, especially because it now sometimes takes two people to change Lucy when she's feeling like streaking.

Lucy was doing just this last week when Adam and I decided to give her a bath. The sound of running water inspired her, and she wet all over me. Before I had a child, being peed on would have gone on my list of 10 Things I Will Never Stand For. Now, though, I stood for it. And I didn't stop standing until Lucy was in the tub, Adam was bathing her, and it was safe for me to change pants. Along with many other gross things, getting peed on is a lot better than watching a lot of stuff that they show on TV and in the newspaper.

And this brings me to the bottom line of parenthood. Once you become one, you invariably hear a story about something awful happening to someone else's child. And then, before you know it, you find yourself blinking back tears, because you can understand someone else's pain in a way you never could before. This is where the day stops for a moment, and you cross your heart and pray that nothing ever happens to your child.

Everything else about being a parent you can learn on the way—the patience, the acceptance, the laughter in the face of chaos and depravity. But that one lesson is the hardest: how to live with the knowledge that the best thing you've ever known—the best part of you, really—will soon be walking. And eventually, she'll walk places you can't protect her.

Are you ready for that? Can anyone ever be?

Clash of the Parents

While lying in bed, I started thinking about the difference between mothers and fathers. This wasn't just idle contemplation. On the contrary, I was lying in a patch of cookie crumbs, and the topic naturally came to mind.

"Adam, wake up," I said. "How did crumbs get in the sheets?"

"Oh," he said. "Lucy must have forgotten she had a cookie."

A cookie in bed? This, I realized, is half the difference between mothers and fathers.

Here's how it happened. I had taken a rare night off—just the third one since Lucy was born nearly a year ago. Adam, Lucy, and I had traveled to Whistler, British Columbia, for a wedding. The night before the ceremony, the women all went out to dinner together while the "menfolk" tended the "cheeruns." (That's how the groom described it, anyway— menfolk and cheeruns. And to think, he grew up in New Jersey.)

Tending cheeruns apparently requires putting them to bed with cookies. When I came home, I found Lucy passed out. Her arms were flung out to either side, and she wore the serene mask of deep sleep. I didn't know about the forgotten cookie until I was all tucked in myself, on top of the many crumbs it had shed escaping Lucy's grip. And I didn't find it until the next morning when I was making the bed. It popped out, a sad little disk all gnawed around the edges.

Naturally, I ate it.

This is the other half of the difference between mothers and fathers. Dads put babies to bed with cookies. Moms sleep in the crumbs, and then eat the wounded hunks their children have discarded. I draw the line when it comes to food bits that find their way into her diapers. But my scavenging technique has saved me precious time in the morning. Why make breakfast, when there's a perfectly good source of nutrition in the crib, the high chair, the car seat, and baby's little overall pockets? Now that I'm thinking of it, it's probably a really good thing I can't reach my own breasts. Who knows what kind of snacking I would have done in these often desperate first months of Lucy's life?

But getting back to nutrition. Adam put Lucy to bed with dessert. This is not something I would ever do. And it's not just because it will rot her perfect little teeth, though that is one very good reason to avoid the practice. Rather, a slept-on cookie just doesn't make a great breakfast for me. If I'm going to put Lucy to bed with anything, it ought to be a pot of coffee and a scone. But I wouldn't trust her to leave me with any leftovers. So for now, I hand Lucy to Adam with clean teeth and a hug. And then he performs the magic ritual, something I would never have the patience to do.

It goes like this: Adam changes Lucy's diaper and puts her in her jammies. Next they say good night to everything on the second floor of our house. They say good night to the pictures on the walls. They say good night to my T-shirts, and good night to the lamp that's still in the closet because we don't have a bedside table to put it on. They say good night to babies Number One, Two, Three, and Four, who make appearances in various mirrors between the bedroom and bathroom. They rustle the shower curtain, and bid it sweet dreams. They say good night to the computer, and to each stuffed animal in Lucy's room. Then they read a book or two. Then Lucy and Adam come downstairs and say good night to me. Often, I nurse Lucy a little bit, and then return her to Adam, who takes her upstairs to do the whole routine over again.

About thirty minutes after he's started, Adam comes down with empty arms. I could never do something like this every night, let alone even once. I would never think to say good night to the shower curtain. I also don't have the patience to coax her to sleep. My thought process goes more like this: Babies need sleep. You're a baby. You should go to sleep, or I will fail you as a parent. Also, if I put you to bed with a cookie, your teeth will rot. And I will fail you as a parent. Excuse me while I toss myself out your window.

Adam is the creative, patient one who invents all the voices for the stuffed animals. I am the one who focuses on such boring things as tooth enamel, sleep requirements, sunscreen, immunizations, nutrition, and general crud removal. I suppose our roles could just as easily be switched, assuming I could for more than twelve seconds let go of my Catholic guilt complex and Protestant work ethic.

For now, I'm happy to let Adam be the fun one. That could be because Lucy lets me know all the time that she needs me. She doesn't say, "Hey. Thanks for looking out for my teeth" or anything like that. But when she falls and bonks her head, I'm the one she stretches her arms toward. When she wakes up from a nap, she doesn't smile until I'm holding her. And she will cry, guaranteed, if I put her down before she's had her fill.

Adam got a little taste last week of what it's like to be the necessary parent. He took Lucy to the aquarium, because he thought it would be fun for her to watch the seals eat. In retrospect, this was a bad idea. Lucy got one look at the frogmen who were gliding around underwater doling out fish parts, and she had a panic attack. Adam says she crawled up his shoulder and clutched his head. Only the much smaller, much cuter sea otters restored her.

"It felt really good to be the one she wanted," Adam told me later.

I knew what he meant. And someday, when he's the one grilling her boyfriends in the living room, maybe I can be the fun one. Then again, maybe not. All those teenage boys want the same thing—to be in extreme proximity to Lucy's perfect, perfect teeth. The mere thought of it makes me want to stick another cookie in her crib.

Getting a Life

Lucy Is One

Lucy turned one on Sunday. I had her all to myself for a while in the morning, because Adam needed just twenty more minutes of sleep—twenty minutes that turned into an hour, but that is another story altogether. As Lucy scurried around the carpet, playing with the cardboard boxes her new toys came in, I started leaking a few tears. I can't believe a year has passed. It's been the longest of years, and the shortest of years. It's been the best of times. I suppose I could steal from Dickens and say it's also been the worst of times. But that wouldn't be true.

During the last year, I feel like I've been a part of a miracle. A child has come into our lives, from no place I could see or feel. We watched her move on ultrasound. I felt her kick and tumble inside me. We held her when she could not lift her head. We cheered when she rolled over the first time. We propped her up with pillows so she could sit and see the world from new heights. And we gasped with wonder, delight, and fear when she started pulling herself up in the crib.

And now here she is, a year old, flipping through her *Touch and Feel Puppy* book, and barking like a dog. When Adam finally came downstairs, roused by the very loud "educational" toy phone, we talked a little about the baby woofing at our feet.

"She's so alive," he said. And really, that sums it up so well. She's alive. This is what stings my eyes every time I think of it—that something so beautiful and difficult, someone so fragile and so resilient is cruising around the living room, trying so very hard to grab a handful of cat. From the cat's perspective, all of this is a pain in the tail. And if I didn't stop every once in a while to catch my breath, I can see myself thinking the same: that a baby is a real pain in the tail. The work is endless, unglamorous, and messy.

But this is why I need to take a break every now and then. I need to watch the creature who takes so much effort, and to be amazed that she's here. I try to do this every day. It makes me feel as though I have a front-row seat at the world's most ancient and mysterious show, that I am witness to the dawn of time. I'm sure all of this hovering and weeping will annoy Lucy when she's, say, eighteen. But I don't think I'll be able to restrain myself.

Since I've become a mother, I have been transformed. Part of the change was the shock of having a helpless creature under my twenty-four-hour care. This is something I adjusted to pretty quickly, mainly as a side effect of "the stupiding." The stupiding occurs when new parents lose so many brain cells to sleep deprivation that we no longer remember the feeling of leaving the house carrying just a wallet and keys, and the very simple life that implies. Signs of this disorder include putting frozen vegetables in the cupboard, losing all the frills in your vocabulary, and for Adam, attempting to brush his teeth with a razor. If you can't remember how easy your life used to be, the drudgery of caring for an infant is much, much easier.

The more significant change took a lot longer for me to understand. Unlike the stupiding, which is physical, this one is emotional. Having a child helped me value my own life much, much more. For starters, I waste much less time. When you watch how quickly a baby goes from being a help-less infant to a near-toddler who understands you when you say "Show me a star," you realize that the speed of life is swift, indeed. Every day for Lucy is a day where she learns some-thing new, where she experiences something for the first time, where she takes the unfamiliar and explores it.

She has inspired me to do the same. It used to be that I had dreams for how I wanted my life to be—and how I would be, if only I had the time. Now, I am much better at making the time. I dream less, and I do more. For example, I'd spent my entire life wanting to be a writer. I nibbled at the edges of a writing career, but chose safer alternatives because I feared I'd fail. I also didn't think I was really allowed to do what I wanted to do; I'd be a better person if I did what I was sup-posed to do. Only selfish people think they're entitled to pur-sue their dreams, I thought. Once Lucy came along, and once I'd actually pushed an 8-pound baby through the equivalent of a garden hose, I realized that lots of things that seem impossible aren't, if you just keep pushing forward a little at a time.

Then, of course, the fear became, "If I spend time writing, am I cheating Lucy?" This is something every mother who works outside the home—and, I'd bet, every mother who has more than one child, or who does the family laundry—fears. I've learned to dismiss those demons, though. By pursuing a passion and believing in myself, I am showing Lucy how a person makes a dream real, little by little, every day. And this, I have learned, is one of the truly important things for a mother to do.

I also have a different perspective on the people around me. Everyone is somebody's child, somebody's miracle, deserving of love and awe—even the shirtless beggar waving the giant cardboard mug that says, "Why Lie? I Need a Beer." I don't give him any money, of course. His mother wouldn't want me to. But I think of him with compassion every time I drive by, just because once upon a time, he too was a one-year-old crawling around somebody's carpet.

The biggest change, though, is that I no longer take simple blessings for granted. Before I had Lucy, most of what happened to me was within my control. Now, however, the things I care about most—her health, her happiness—aren't. In the last year, I've seen close friends suffer through a miscarriage. One of my mother's colleagues lost her newborn to Down's syndrome. Another friend's mother is being treated for ovarian cancer. And yet, here I am, graced with a beautiful, healthy, funny, and intelligent baby, a kind and supportive husband, and plenty of writing challenges that make me excited to go to work every day (even if it's just in a sweltering room the size of a closet). It's when I realize how lucky I've been that I feel equally responsible to make the most of it—to take the energy that this realization has created and to use it for some good, wherever I see an opportunity.

Though I sometimes wonder how some people end up waving cardboard beer mugs, while others end up happy and rich with love and hope and dreams, I'm doing my best not to worry yet about the distant future. If you think only of what's far off, you run a good risk of missing the magic along the way. Keeping a journal has inspired me to notice what Lucy does. It's also helped me to remember it later, when exhaustion otherwise might have erased that part of my brain. Inevitably, I missed some of the fun of this first year. But not much. And I'll always have it with me.

I read a quotation recently in a collection of essays by E. B. White that captures some of what I'm feeling:

"When my wife's Aunt Caroline was in her nineties, she lived with us and she once remarked: 'Remembrance is sufficient of the beauty we have seen.' I cherish the remembrance of the beauty I have seen. I cherish the grave, compulsive world."

In just that way, I cherish the memory of Lucy's transformation from mysterious infant to understood child. Take the memory, for example, of Lucy's expression when Adam held her birthday cake in front of her. Her face glowed in the light of the lone candle burning atop the tiny, pink cake. We sang our best Happy Birthday song to her. But instead of looking happy, her face said, "How awful! I'm the only one here who doesn't know the lyrics!" She didn't really know what to do with the cake, either. We put her in her high chair, and set the cake in front of her. She leaned forward and started biting it, tentatively.

So much for the Hollywood-style birthday cake smash.

Lucy handled her first birthday as she handles other new and unfamiliar things. She's an observer. She doesn't like to do something unless she's sure it's going to work. She was like this with talking, and she is the same way with walking. She's taken steps, but only at our urging. Otherwise, she prefers to crawl, or to cruise in the safe shadow of the living room furniture. The more she does, the more I start to understand the person she is, and the kind of mother I need to be to help her have a full and happy life—one where caution is balanced with courage.

Just thinking about it, I am once again in tears. How quickly this goes by. How magical it is to watch.

And how good it feels to love this much.